Themes on a Variation

Also by Edwin Morgan from Carcanet

Rites of Passage: Selected Translations (1976)
The New Divan (1977)
Poems of Thirty Years (1982)
Selected Poems (1985)

EDWIN MORGAN

Themes on a Variation

CARCANET

Acknowledgements

Acknowledgements are due to: *Antaeus, Fox, Beloit Poetry Journal, Dalhousie Review, Not Just Another Pile of Bricks, Ethos, Verse, Word and Image, Dream, Strawberry Fare, The Green Book, London Review of Books, Lines Review, The News, The North, Stride, Conjunctions, Poetry Book Society Anthology 1987, Poems for Shakespeare 1987, With a Poet's Eye* (Tate Gallery Anthology). *Sonnets from Scotland* was published by Mariscat Press in 1984. *From the Video Box* was published by Mariscat Press in a limited edition in 1986. Acknowledgement is due to the concept of the Video Box, where viewers can record their reactions to television programmes, as shown in Gus MacDonald's Channel 4 programme, 'Right to Reply'. *Newspoems* was published in a limited edition by Wacy! Publications in 1987. In December 1986 Edwin Morgan and Peter McCarey began 'reconstructing' some fairly well-known poems. The series was initiated by Peter McCarey, who worked first on each poem, Edwin Morgan countering with his own contribution; the whole sequence was published in *Verse* (4.2). Edwin Morgan's half is reprinted here pp. 42-8.

First published in 1988 by
Carcanet Press Limited
208-212 Corn Exchange Buildings
Manchester M4 3BQ

British Library Cataloguing in Publication Data

Morgan, Edwin
    Themes on a variation.
    I. Title
    821'.914   PR6063.069

    ISBN 0-85635-778-2

The publisher acknowledges financial assistance
from the Arts Council of Great Britain

Typeset in 10pt Palatino by Bryan Williamson, Manchester
Printed in England by SRP Ltd, Exeter

To M.T.

At present we have *glasnost* leading to *perestroika*; in future we shall have *perestroika* leading to *glasnost*.

Julian Semyonov

Contents

The Dowser (1986)   11
Variations on Omar Khayyám (1984)   12
Stanzas (1986)   16
The Room (1985)   22
Dear man, my love goes out in waves (1987)   23
Waking on a Dark Morning (1986)   24
The Gurney (1986)   27
The Bench (1985)   28
Nineteen Kinds of Barley (1984)   30
A Trace of Wings (1985)   32
The Hanging Gardens of Babylon (1982)   33
A Bobbed Sonnet for Code Cobber (1986)   35
The Computer's First Birthday Card (1966)   36
Byron at Sixty-Five (1985)   37
Shakespeare: a Reconstruction (1986)   42
To the Queen: a Reconstruction (1987)   43
Chillon: a Reconstruction (1987)   45
True Ease in Writing: a Reconstruction (1987)   46
On Time: a Reconstruction (1987)   47
Not Marble: a Reconstruction (1987)   48
Halley's Comet (1985)   49
The Gorbals Mosque (1984)   50
Rules for Dwarf-Throwing (1986)   51
The Bear (1987)   52
Save the Whale Ball (1981)   53
Dom Raja (1986)   55
The Change (1987)   57
Vereshchagin's Barrow (1982)   58

Newspoems (1965-1971)
   Holy Flying Saucer Satori   63
   The Computer's First Translation   64
   Cain Said   65
   Notice in Hell   66
   Notice in Heaven   67
   The Commonest Kind   68
   Sick Man   69

Joe's Bar   70
Early Days for Dr Moreau   71
Hex   72
In Mid-Trepan   73
Hooked   74
Charon's Song   75
Epitaph   76
Legend   77
Revolt of the Elements   78
Revolt of the Objects   79
Hair-raising   80
Apple Girl   81
O for a Life of Sensations   82
Cooked   83
Beckford Heard a Voice Saying   84
Forgetful Duck   85
Said the Pigeon   86
Pigeons: Elizabethan   87
Car Goes Ape   88
Möbius's Bed   89
Come In Old Cock   90
Idyll   91
Caedmon's Second Hymn   92
New English Riddles: 1   93
New English Riddles: 2   94
Ballad 13   95
Scrumwear   96
Talk About Camp   97
Hypermarine   98
Ball   99
Scotland Enters the Common Market   100
Advice to a Corkscrew   101
An Unpublished Poem by Zukofsky   102
Unpublished Poems by Creeley: 1   103
Unpublished Poems by Creeley: 2   104
Unpublished Poems by Creeley: 3   105
Unpublished Poems by Creeley: 4   106
Unpublished Poems by Creeley: 5   107
Unpublished Poems by Creeley: 6   108
Concrete Ballad of Reading Gaol   109

Visual Soundpoem   110
Found Concrete Poem: The Enactment   111
In Silhouette   112

From the Video Box (1986)   115

Sonnets from Scotland (1984)
  Slate   141
  Carboniferous   141
  Post-Glacial   142
  In Argyll   142
  The Ring of Brodgar   143
  Silva Caledonia   143
  Pilate at Fortingall   144
  The Mirror   144
  The Picts   145
  Colloquy in Glaschu   145
  Memento   146
  Matthew Paris   146
  At Stirling Castle, 1507   147
  Thomas Young, M.A. (St Andrews)   147
  Lady Grange on St Kilda   148
  Theory of the Earth   148
  Poe in Glasgow   149
  De Quincey in Glasgow   149
  Peter Guthrie Tait, Topologist   150
  G.M. Hopkins in Glasgow   150
  1893   151
  The Ticket   151
  North Africa   152
  Caledonian Antisyzygy   152
  Travellers (1)   153
  Travellers (2)   153
  Seferis on Eigg   154
  Matt McGinn   154
  Post-Referendum   155
  Gangs   155
  After a Death   156
  Not the Burrell Collection   156
  1983   157

A Place of Many Waters   157
The Poet in the City   158
The Norn (1)   158
The Norn (2)   159
The Target   159
After Fallout   160
The Age of Heracleum   160
Computer Error: Neutron Strike 161
Inward Bound   161
The Desert   162
The Coin   162
The Solway Canal   163
A Scottish Japanese Print   163
Outward Bound   164
On Jupiter   164
Clydegrad   165
A Golden Age   165
The Summons   166

The Dowser

With my forked branch of Lebanese cedar
I quarter the dunes like downs and guide
an invisible plough far over the sand.
But how to quarter such shifting acres
when the wind melts their shapes, and shadows
mass where all was bright before,
and landmarks walk like wraiths at noon?
All I know is that underneath,
how many miles no one can say,
an unbroken water-table waits
like a lake; it has seen no bird or sail
in its long darkness, and no man;
not even pharaohs dug so far
for all their thirst, or thirst of glory,
or thrust-power of ten thousand slaves.
I tell you I can smell it though,
that water. I am old and black
and I know the manners of the sun
which makes me bend, not break. I lose
my ghostly footprints without complaint.
I put every mirage in its place.
I watch the lizard make its lace.
Like one not quite blind I go
feeling for the sunken face.
So hot the days, the nights so cold,
I gather my white rags and sigh
but sighing step so steadily
that any vibrance in so deep
a lake would never fail to rise
towards the snowy cedar's bait.
Great desert, let your sweetness wake.

Variations on Omar Khayyám

1

The caravan-master rose and clapped his hands.
The camel-men dashed out their coffee-dregs,
cracked whips, cried, cracked jokes, slapped, coaxed,
loaded, prodded; the beasts rose, groaned,
unknelt, rocked upright, stood, snaked their necks,
showed their teeth, splayed their toes,
softly stamped the cool dawn sand.
The master strapped on his gauntlet, his falcon flapped,
he spoke to it, it shook its bell, he strode, the whole
long line swayed off, set out, awake, slow, cheerful, steady,
robes loose, mongrels yapping, brasses bright,
banter of women, jingle of bangles, till the sun rose

and fed on them from red to orange, orange
to yellow, yellow to white, swallowed
the last black distant dots and filled the screen
where they had filed past, almost like life,
in close-up or in long-shot, wound off a reel
in the dark archive bay. Outside the ship
asteroids sparkled, hurtled; behind it the train
of its flotilla swung past Mars, all space
its battered caravanserai. The crews were wild,
half-trained, had stashed tequila, zithers, mescal,
hamsters, revolvers, the captain had macaws with headphones,
a cook was ejected, exploded, but still the majestic
tattered drove tried the universe.
Burnt-out computers, pushed from airlocks like blackheads,
made a cindertrack across another screen
as the convoy diminished and disappeared

and that panel flickered, not crowded round
by angels, not in heaven, but hung one moment
in annihilation's waste, the console glowed
unplayed by fingers, the code changed
every instant, a cold wind hurried down the steps
and ruffled the fresh dark well of life;
to taste it, drink from it, human lips

will do if they will not hold back,
but they must hurry, they must run,
we must run with our thirst,
all must hurry with their water-skins,
all must not knock but go,
all must slake and store,
throats, pitchers, all we have
and that is not enough,
when stars are setting, and the well
brims one moment, and the caravan
starts out for the dawn
of nothing, nothing at all.

2

A hand rose above the marshes near Basra,
high and bold over the broken land.
Everyone saw it, there was no hiding it.
A cloud of mortar smoke? No no,
it formed itself too perfectly,
though none could agree on its colour.
It held nothing – what could it hold? –
but made as if to write, on that dark blue.
We saw its fingers crouch, and move,
and thought a cordite-haunted sky had little need
of messages, or any of the rolling dead young men
awash in the shallows, gassed in foxholes,
burnt at despairing angles, left for film-crews.
Shi'a against Shi'a? Ideology
makes good dust, fills in mass graves.
No message then? Q is not N,
and never think it is either, in this world:
every iota, hamza, shibboleth
burrs the graver, snags the plane; rules.
What will you grow on scorched homelands,
brother? Scorched homelands, after a while.

The dead roll still. The moving finger writes,
moves on. It made an error? It
did not understand you? It

missed the background? What,
you want to lure it back, you want it
to rewrite – changes – ever so slight –
glosses – is that it? Or you think it
wrote like Satan from left to right: what,
up there? in space? Or you object
a text so bald cannot be pious? What if piety
is a vulture on the roof of a torture-chamber?
You will not alter half a line,
not half a word, of that high text,
that bald text, not half a letter
that has been written in that text.

Ah but those in veils, at tombs, have tears.
Is there not a figure of pity
moving like a half-seen shadow
under the windows of those waiting
for a letter, for a step?
There is a package of effects
with no pity; closed doors; only smothered cries
are safe. Wishes
would turn back time. The martyrs
stiffened on the mudflats at night,
were long unburied. Mother and wife
re-read the official word. If they should weep
for ever, they would not wash out that word,
but they must never weep for ever.

3

Disengage, and lie back each upon the sand
as we have done so many times and may do yet.
The desert like a breathing animal
burns and grows cold, burns and grows cold,
until one day we find its cold as unremitting
as our own, while the lizard warms his blood
above us unseen. Bind the place then
with marram grass, or do not, it is as good
to trudge to wells without a cumber and let

custom carry the jar to its cool zarf.
Markers for sultans, vanishing for us.

But lying back in the quick twilight we stopped
shading the sun with our arms, and shivered.
It really was a wilderness, and the solitary spring
made it no less, nor the gaunt scrub. Women in black
took water beyond the horizon. If you tire of me,
talk to scorpions. – When I tire of you,
scorpions will talk. – I know; it was a joke.
– Never joke about the desert. Let's have a fire.
We made a fire; the stars came out.
We had a loaf of bread left, we clouded up
some pungent arak with well-water, and you began
singing that wild wavering raucous song
that seemed to tell the planets, Here we are!
Vanishing is not for us! As the fire sputtered
I crackled it into joy with more sticks,
an old piece of harness, some half-buried pages
from a lost book: the curling letters
curled again in fire, and warmed us.
– Cover me. – What? – I said, Cover me.
Not the rug. Dear God. Cover me!
Shaft me, I want all that darkness.
I want to feel everything till I feel nothing.
I want to fix the Great Bear for good
with love.

The wilderness
seemed to lift us first in its stony arms,
then further higher we were on its back
between stony wings, never fled but slowly soared,
hovered, the unbelievable heaviness
rocking us with light ease. There is no paradise
(who could believe in such shadows?) but
what there is can be so nearly so
I'd give the wilderness no other name
if you were there. There is no paradise
but you, that's all I know, here or to come.

15

Stanzas

1

How can I love you, is there any way?
The rain that almost drove the windows in
as November left the world
had nothing in its bluster left to say
but: warm in room need never roam to win.

You let me kiss you, but your silent arms
are by your side, but what I wrap is warm
and does not struggle there,
but au revoirs at doors are powerless charms,
but still you shoulder to me through the storm.

So I twist and turn, now on, now back.
Relentless quartz hums on the mantelpiece.
Well, we have had our times,
I ought to be content, but any lack
love feels is incompatible with peace.

The lack, and so the love itself, are fed
from your eyes; they look at me in ways
I have no words for, where
something hidden half smiles, half hoods its head,
totally haunts my unresisting days.

Your red hair in the doorway is like fire.
My arms are loath to let your kindness go,
but I must turn the latch.
You are warm as a bird, as a deer, as desire.
I look at you this time. I know you know.

2

I was thirty-eight when you were born.
You think I want a son? Of course I do –
or daughter – but that's not it,
not it at all. I'd rather have your scorn
than you should never know what runs me through –

yourself, you are the blade, the freeing light
that cuts imagined age to shreds, and doubts
from veins, and solitude
away, quite altogether, cuts day and night
until there's just eternity, and shouts

of wakened earthbound sleepers, metal horns
making cracks in doomed ramparts, songs
as tough as tundra, sails
tearing doldrums apart like white-hot thorns,
the chrysalis of rights, the dying wrongs –

I can never shrink back, I tell you that,
you've drawn me out on such an instant thread
I'm like a flower, sunned,
turning, glowing, thrusting the grubby tat
of rootedness deep in the garden bed

so we can soar if we should want to soar,
or make a marigold of the whole air,
of that entire bright place,
where pungent perfumes never known before
would wind the world up through them like a stair.

3

To be simple, to be clear, to be true –
the sweat and cost of it are surely such
that all must shut up shop.
Why buy, then sell, what metaphor can do?
What shoulder did metaphors ever touch?

I don't know; you're confusing me; come on.
Of course a poem doesn't seize lapels,
but can it seize the soul?
And if it does, why should comparison
not flush the ripples of a brace of bells

and flood the bays and oxbows of our hearts?
And where do these bells come from? How should I
know – carried in the wind –
I heard them, ice-cream vans, carols, parts
of dashboard Messiaen, churches even, why

can there not be bells in cities, no need
to skulk a provenance, any more than ask
the moon on Primrose Hill
if it was sailing at its cloudy speed
to see two sleepers sprawled without a mask.

All the same, it was simple to wake, to dress.
Good coffee, orange, rolls – is that not clear?
And only what is true
is harder, just a little, I confess,
except that happiness was hovering near.

4

They are not good, thoughts of the shortest day.
A vicious intermittent frequent sleet
turning to rain, not snow,
thickens from the low gloomy array
of cloud and squelches under hurrying feet.

Northern peoples take it as it comes
and even in the grey of noon can see
signs of the light that waits;
but now I only feel it as it numbs,
for you go home to him, and I to me.

Ring road buses hiss and lurch through slush,
churn kerbside mud and camouflage the street
with lumbering zebra'd drab.
The afternoon closes, and wraps the crush
of hunching anoraks and hurrying feet.

How different was that motorway return,
hour after hour, to talk, laugh, doze, to be
ourselves, clear evening, moon
and lighted towns all running like a burn:
but you went home to him, and I to me.

The darkest day at last deserts the year.
How can the sun and this earth ever meet?
I seem not to know that,
or how the fading of one haunting fear
could rid my nightmare of its hurrying feet.

Buffeted by every visit you make
I clutch the flying shrouds of reason, but
I need you more and more,
and anything that for resistance' sake
was rock is seething foam and floating strut.

Sometimes if we should hug or briefly cling
or lean, it is as if a furnace roared
to melt me down again
and forty years have slipped off like a ring
too tight, too gold, for this love to afford.

For it would be the simplest cost of all
if you would come to me in that exchange
no one could lose from, bind,
or stumble over, or ever miscall,
but of such a release, such ease, such range

we would ourselves be in a ring of joy
and rainbow the rough waters bright above
the earth as under it:
one springing circle linking star, bay, buoy
and the half-charted under-world of love –

love that rules, whatever we may say,
taking us to peaks and troughs new-found
where we may praise our stars
or plead on our bent knees against them, grey
hair or red, gone to earth, green as the ground.

6

The year dissolves in solid days of rain,
runs out, runs off with everything except
you, what you brought me,
gave without having to give, the pain
of the lit fire, the drawn resin that wept.

And I would have nothing other than that.
How the story will end, I cannot see.
You must take stock, take stock!
says the old year. I've scrubbed; shaken the mat;
changed calendars; touch of paint; house, so. But me?

I would have nothing other than what has changed.
You have peeled off some covering, some coat
I thought I needed, when
all I needed was to see it gone, estranged,
not mine, not me. I settled and I wrote

those lines, these lines, only to be true.
Let us be level-headed! With the head?
The head is like a bird,
all quick, hot, hungry, darting through the blue
or two eyes in a rainbush, shivering, unfed –

alive though! We live, we feel, we know
the truth's in feeling, and the openness
feeling must give at last.
Come on then buzz my door and shake the snow
from your padded jacket if January whiteness

drives wetness away; come in; the kettle's on,
the books are out, I die for your look, your talk.
You see how easy I am.
Good God how that Chalk Farm moon knocked and shone!
Have you not tried my heart? It has no lock.

The Room

After René Magritte, *Souvenir de voyage III* (1951)

It was a blustery March day in the mountains
when she told him they had come to the end of the story,
she would not see him again, he should take a job
in the next village. As she looked up at him,
holding her hair back from her eyes, he shuddered
at a determination nothing would tug her from.
Daffodils bowed; twigs raced past; the sky
was in a ferment. She tugged her coat
and turned back quickly along the street.

He ran from that place, pounded the craggy paths,
threw oaths after the loose stones he kicked
into the chasm, choked back exclamations
the wind did not cut first. Abandonment
drove him forward and flew before him.
Blindly he made the straggling lower village,
slowed down, kept silent, picked an inn.
'Here is the key. You'll find the room all right,
on the first floor.' The dusty stairs seemed endless,
the landing clock could hardly bring itself
to tick, the greasy air he groped through
had gone viscous as at last he gripped the key
and slowly ground its tons of metal home.

And the room waited for the jilted man
to join it, for its life, like his, had stopped.
Its bare floor-boards, table, thick damask cloth
were already half-fossilized, and the same rock
they were becoming had invaded the book,
the bowl of fruit, the bottle and its glass.
Stone shutters opened on an airless world
of stone that pressed its twisted pinnacles
almost into the room. What balcony,
what garden, what sky? There was nothing
unpetrified, uncracked, unpitted, pitied.

Only the lock is not stone: slowly it turns.

22

'Dear man, my love goes out in waves'

Dear man, my love goes out in waves
and breaks. Whatever is, craves.
Terrible the cage
to see all life from, brilliantly about,
crowds, pavements, cars, or hear the common shout
of goals in a near park.
But now the black bars arc
blue in my breath – split – part –
I'm out – it's art,
it's love, it's rage –

Standing in rage in decent air
will never clear the place of care.
Simply to be
should be enough, in the same city, and let
absurd despair tramp and roar off-set.
Be satisfied with it,
the gravel and the grit
the struggling eye can't lift,
the veils that drift,
the weird to dree.

Press close to me at midnight as
you say goodbye; that's what it has
to offer, life
I mean. Into the frost with you; into
the bed with me; and get the light out too.
Better to shake unseen
and let real darkness screen
the shadows of the heart,
the vacant part-
ner, husband, wife.

Waking on a Dark Morning

1

If anything was ever even as at ease
As where they lay when it had made a scene
All but overgrown, a sole drop lost at once,
Whatever even took it from the wood
Prevaricating, although slowly, like to bounce
As clouds of clay could, thrown not to stick,
And gravity keeping a low profile might
Low even, rolling along to be milked
Of such leaden showers as can bear it,
Even for ever, even without the deference
Of a long arm, within interstices
However bright, ceilings however blue,
To carry ends however plain, if so,
It could do nothing for dry eyes, no,
Not even when they were raised right up, or closed
To run the moon's grey pack into the ground.

2

It is hardly impossible not to speak out,
Yet everyone thinks it is foolhardy to speak in.
Whatever way you come at it it goes.
The perch for anything that flies flies.
Whenever there was a void there was a move
Till everything fell forward and was seen gone.
Those that thought it was something, hardly more,
Bungled or not, blundered about all night
Till there was nothing gracious that had hardly crumbled
Before a wizening-up was seen never to be impossible
As long as nothing could change otherwise,
For all its blowzy bluster. To be winged,
Lying, a shout more than ever unheard,
With anything blood could speak, they knew better,
And the smoke was only curling into nothing
When things that might have made a ring were silent.

3

Every shot is dumped, for all the flare.
They imagined nothing like survivors,
The arrow was to keep in its side, the earth
Being as ready as it had always been.
Even if it was slow, they wanted it.
Their plumes are petrified into the causeway.
What armourers are at large for, august though it is,
Needed even less singing in its veins
When the dogs passed over like a wavering banner
Someone had sewn something darker in
Than any night it streamed through. For the fire,
No one who never saw it ever knew
What solemn canopies, melting in swags,
Were crowns, or jewels dropped on cheeks like eyes
Were only that, or ever felt the weight
Of one intolerable iron veil.

4

Even what was struggled for, if there,
Was anybody's, hardly more than the dark
But felt as smoke or mud or fog or fur,
While open-windowed curtains breathed like gills,
Half-seen in worlds half-thought, in seas half-sailed,
For anyone believes a heavy sheet,
And it was almost very cold, or colder;
Old glaciers new as they lurched inches, metres
Into the sound; nothing is far away; it snored,
The blowhole. Wherever they dived they thought
It could never really, or hardly ever, be darker,
Yet bands of it charged them, unrelenting,
Not even ever what they knew, not blinding them
But sending them all bound like mummies upward
Right into what could only laugh at drowners
Shouting to swim without a leg or arm.

5

No, it was only one; in the dream two,
In the nightmare many. The sleeper still sketched
His groaning wraiths in shapes of stars and seals
Though nothing ever shot an autumn sky
Or mewed, whatever might have been half-human
Or might have blazed and crashed or cradled omens
Was in the process, off the process, the profound
Could only ever even think it sounded.
Jetsam of a crumpled dogfish sea-purse,
The sleeper's pillow gave an ear a jolt,
A rasp of rusty sandpaper, his skin
Bled down the bed clasped by such last shagreen
As the most grave and desperate sharks of daybreak
Laboured to give, and any knew it was,
Whatever might be thought of dawn, like care,
Or pain, or even horror, not never, but now.

6

It was an early bus that wakened me,
Braking at the stop outside my window.
The thin curtains filtered an amazing light,
Half red, half silver-grey, into the room.
The amaryllis on the sill seemed ready
To take off with a cry, a bird the shadows
Were slipping from, and every last concealment.
I yawned, and stretched out like a starfish.
Memory threw up streaks of something dark.
I found I did not even want to know.
How quick the deadly shades are, to crowd back
As if they could not stand a waking man!
The night never wanted me to speak, did it?
But speak we will, and clearly too. The great
Rude day strides the roofs to rouse me. Rouse too
The friend I love who makes his star elsewhere!

The Gurney

A gaunt, wasted, childlike bag of bones
was all they had to wheel in on the gurney.
One lover, one van-driver were all the procession.
They found a cardboard box marked ROCK HUDSON,
bundled the body in, slung the box on to the cot,
ran with it as pressmen banged the crematorium doors,
rolled their bungled parcel straight into the oven
and watched it burn so fast that the very body
was nothing, as its dignity was, as we all may be,
in an instant. No camera recorded
what can be written. Everyone needs someone,
when cot and box are waiting for their journey.

The Bench

After Tom Phillips, *Benches*

Honey-brown varnish glistens: Easter hymn.
Even its WET PAINT sign sings out spring's here.
It's sturdy, foursquare, brown, abstract, and clear.
Nothing could make the backdrop tree buds dim
or undo wonder from the sharp fresh green
of daffodil strikes but this silent thing
that sits and shouts, a throne to kid a king,
and when he rises, nakedness is seen.
But nothing sticks except a twig, dropped there
by frenziedly building crows. The March wind
tugs at it, but it will not stir, or mar
perfection less by letting the air bare
its print. No caws, no nest, no brood is thinned.
The first to brush the twig off sees the scar.

One thing is certain, it is not abstract.
Who can see the wooden slats for five, six
people, a dog (seven!), pigeons, a mix
of life as warm in its midsummer fact
and midday pause as ever hit a park
with one moment withdrawn from every pain?
Crackle of crisps lost in hot blue space, brain
at a drowsy crossword, crumbs in an ark
of fingers held out (holy that too!) as
treasures for motley wings and scavengers,
mingled with 'I don't know, that's what he said –'
and '– wants one of those instant cameras'
and '– a nice bit of ham –'; those passengers
race in their happiness towards the dead.

Leaves die, but not the tree, not yet, not soon.
Red, yellow, crinkled, papery, they scrape
along the bench, collect at the slumped shape
of a tramp; they've nothing to say; forenoon,
afternoon he sleeps, stirs, shifts, mutters, feels
October probing sluggish arteries,
clutches his coat like a cloak. Batteries
of sleet wait to be loosed, not yet. With squeals
cut by rising gusts, children chase and dart.
There is a thud of chestnuts, and one breaks.
What a soft sheeny tender eye looks out
in wonder from its shattered shell! Take heart
it says. The old man stares at it. The rakes
rattle in sheds, there is a far-off shout –

never heard in the whiteness over all
and the seat quite filled with high-drifted snow
like a dust-sheeted hurdy-gurdy. Go
by it still, good winter walkers! The fall
of silent feet dislodges a few grains.
Whistle and breath might melt a dozen more.
But suddenly all flakes are in uproar:
a great floundering setter coughs and strains
and leaves his lead, flounces onto the bench
through wet white flying sprays and veils, and skids
wild claws along the wood at last, shakes, barks,
a snowdog breaking bonds, his boisterous wrench
shows sage winter callow. With white eyelids
he grins; his master laughs. They see lambs, larks.

Nineteen Kinds of Barley

Acclaim was one of eighty thousand waving and bristling in the stadium; his ears crackled in the squeezing heat as he moved with the surge.

Celt was a harp of cobwebs; when they plucked him in the morning he yielded creaks and shivers, a scrape of pure mildew.

Corgi grew up on aircraft steps but never rooted well; his dwarfish habit came from too much handling.

Delta was seldom tracked down; she ran like quicksilver through the monsoons and left an India of children thrusting spears at the sun.

Doublet was woven tight and velvety and pulsed like a heart; they cut him down with pikes.

Flare came suddenly, like a moor-burn, a royal flush, a tenth wave; wild airs and rounded clouds jostled to solicit him.

Golden Promise shook his spiky hair and straddled the shore; cows' tongues rasped his belly when he turned white with salt.

Gold Marker strode over the hill's flank unfurling his strawy banner next to the hot yellow patch of rape; he whistled, and marched like mustard.

Golf had a rough time but grew stoic and hardy; prone on the headland he pricked his ears like flags.

Javelin struck hard and straight through the rain and shone; gloved harvesters swore as the steely beards drew blood and clanked down the chute for robots' bannocks.

Klaxon was so strong he made rutting stags stumble; brewed Thor's mash in Asgard.

Kym leaned lightly, listening; too far off her father Kandym stalked the wastelands, binding and rebinding the restless Kara Kum from his bag of marram.

Lina crouched in a tangled sea of tresses at the feet of Jesus; her roots moaned for the crop they had still to give.

Midas swaggered in a cave-mouth, lolled on couch-grass, played with bear-bones; now gapes, purple, staring, drowned in his seed-hoard.

Nairn was agoraphobic, itched to be malted, doze ten years in casks; a second life under ribs of men.

Natasha bent down her drear dark brows as the thousand-mile-old wind swept to her across the steppe; unbreaking bent down, bowed down, bore unbroken.

Piccolo piped the high meadows awake; his pink-shears gave the dawn chorus an edge.

Themis swayed to the left, to the right, courtly, with all her companions; a chorus of measure, the breathing of the earth, in a windless field.

Vista was a blue-eyed tundra-watcher, hard as nails; when the Yenisei came roaring through her bed she snapped her fingers and cast grain in his face, extending her empire north, towards the ice.

Corn Bunting	shy but perky; haunts fields; grain-scatterer
Reed Bunting	sedge-scuttler; swayer; a cool perch
Cirl Bunting	small whistler; shrill early; find him!
Indigo Bunting	blue darter; like metal; the sheen
Ortolan Bunting	haunts gardens; is caught; favours tables
Painted Bunting	gaudy flasher; red, blue, green; what a whisk!
Snow Bunting	Arctic flyer; ghost-white; blizzard-hardened
Basil Bunting	the sweetest singer; prince of finches; gone from these parts

The Hanging Gardens of Babylon
for John Furnival's 50th birthday

the hanging gravids of babyland
the happy gurgles of bath
the hassle gabblers of gath
the horrible gobblers of broth
the harridan guardians of barchester
the hapless gods of brecht
the hubble gargle of bubble
the hearty gaekwars of baroda
the hatter's gust of blawearie
the hunter's ghost of baskerville
the humming gullies of brum
the hazardous gasps of bellerophon
the heavy glums of brood
the hollow gums of cholmondeley
the hustling grunts of numb
the hungry guzzlers of slough
the hundred groans of caledonia
the hasty grooms of glory
the hallowed grubs of china
the harried gagsters of cuckfield
the hobbling gaffblowers of tirana
the horny golachs of wigtown
the hurricane galleons of duncansby
the hedda gabblers of gloucester
the headless gardeners of kew
the handless gamblers of crewe
the hamfisted gasfitters of hyderabad
the hairy gaddings of sable
the hawthorn gatherers of woodchester
the handheld gardenias of wilts
the hyperactive geotropism of vainglory
the hyacinthine gorgeousness of samson
the holy guns of fun
the halfhearted garters of flannel
the heterogeneous galligaskins of folderol
the harmless gauds of fabulous

the hangdog gadroons of fallopia
the huddled gundogs of fenland
the hagridden gussets of fulvia
the hurdy gurdy of fux
the hidden gleams of furness
the hollied garments of hope
the hengest gleemen of furnivall
the hornbeam glades of fifty
the halcyon galleys of furnival

A Bobbed Sonnet for Code Cobber
for Bob Cobbing's 65th birthday

climbing Popocatepetl with popcorn packets
humming Mahabharata humbly but unhurriedly
surfing through Sargasso with syntagmatic spinnakers
throwing tantrums at Antananarivo train-hoots

Zoroastrian asterisks satirized astutely
Athabaskan aubades ululated unabashed
ro-ro car-wash scrub-up freak-out
tsetse-zizzing isthmus-asthma

onomatopoeic articulation incomparably extrapolated
hubble-bubble hob-nob with heavy-breathing hobos
shaman's-salmon psalm for spawn-master's shawm

slaloming along shalom-hung swan-songs
simply spellbinding spielbonding spoolbending
loading London with logodaedalian lauds

many returns happy
many turns happier
happy turns remain
happy remains turn
turns remain happy
turn happy remains
remains turn happy
mains return happy
happy mains return
main happy returns
main turns happier
happier main turns
happier many turns
many happier turns
many happier turns
many happier turns
er turns er turns ?
happy er er happy ?
er *error* er *check* !
turn er pre turns !
many happy turners
+$?-†!=%0½^´*/£(]&
many gay whistlers
no no no no no no !
many gainsboroughs
stop stop stop stp
happier constables
0101010101010101
raise police pay p
ost early for chri
stmas watch forest
fires get well soo
n bon voyage KRRGK
many happy returns
eh? eh? eh? eh? eh? eh?

Byron at Sixty-Five

The rumour of my death has long abated.
The Greeks still love me, but I don't love Greeks
Except for one – or two; I must be fated
To wander and to change; when the mast creaks
I smell the salt and know my soul unsated
Until it finds the language no man speaks.
And what is that? some simpleton demands
Who's never heard the seething of the sands.

No seething here, though, or not much; the plop
And gurgle of old timbers slowly walloped
By oily steamship wash is not the top
Of pleasure; no sea-horses ever galloped
A winning streak in muck; what made me stop
In Venice? Well, the curtain's nicely scalloped,
My dear contessa's maid has lit a fire,
And shut-out January re-lights desire.

Don't laugh; Childe Harold may be grey and paunchy,
A lame, ex-English, ex-Scottish ex-Romantic
Soon to be ex-everything, including ex-raunchy.
But still I'll have a gaudy night, not frantic
Like forty years ago; and at dawn she
'll re-tell, re-live, forgive each aging antic.
All right, it's comedy; but the comedy's high
You must admit: palazzo, contessa, and I.

Hear how the north wind batters at the pane!
A spot of grog's the thing for nights like this –
Not too much seltzer. Sailors on the main
Have grog for birthdays – victories – and Christmas –
And I'm a sailor – and I've no champagne –
So here's to Doctor Grog, and let's not miss
His therapeutic memories of sails,
And holystoning pigtailed tars, and whales –

Speaking of which, I've just read *Moby-Dick*
And think its author very enigmatic
But enigmatically great, one flick
Of that huge fluke and verse is in the attic,
Prose fills the morning-rooms and thrashes quick
About the hall, large, muscular, and vatic.
We poets must throw off our well-pressed laurels,
Let children play with chinkling beads and corals.

He said. But unresisting, took a rhyme,
Watched the floating bulk of language approach,
Rose up, and at the crucial tilt of time
Shot out that sharp harpoon and saw it broach
The stanza's shoulders to a ship-bell's chime.
And Melville needn't try to drive a coach
And horses through my case in his next book.
He uses metre in his prose, the crook.

But still, America comes on and on,
Land of the turkey, Edgar Allan Poe,
Clam chowder, telegrams, and Audubon.
I think I'll take a tour there, just to know
A New World now that this damned creaky old one
Has got itself a gout in every toe
And totters, more than marches, to the future,
Afraid to break its grim dynastic suture.

What do I care, they'll say, an exiled whiner,
A superannuated stateless has-been.
Victoria's not much of a Regina
In my opinion; let the age come clean,
And stop pretending everything is finer
Because the blood and sweat are seldom seen.
You twitch your skirt, but that still leaves the dust.
You pay, but you don't give, the workhouse crust.

O Forty-Eight, the year of revolutions,
Men on the streets from Budapest to Bradford,
We saw such rhetoric, such resolutions,
So many torchlight columns, but all baffled,

38

All gone into a night without solutions,
And storm-clouds burdening the vengeful scaffold.
Who would not think the tyrants had returned,
And all our boyhood hopes swept up and burned?

Marx and Engels wouldn't; I read their book,
Manifest der Kommunistischen Partei.
They say a spectre's haunting every nook
Of power in Europe, and that chains will fly.
If that is true, the printing-presses shook
Like thunder when these pages flickered by.
Who could believe them? Yet I read it twice,
And thought I heard the cracking of the ice.

I sent a copy off (in German of course)
To Wordsworth, with a pleasing dedication
'To our oldest living renegade'. The force
Of this last-minute well-meant operation
To save his soul proved to be over-coarse,
Or else the man was well beyond salvation.
Soon afterwards, he went to meet his Maker,
An unrepentant stupid Tory Laker.

Peace to all such! as parsons say – not me.
Stir up the fire, Teresa dear, it's dark
And wild outside. Mushrooms, olives, Chianti
Will keep us going in our little ark –
Not so little, I know – that sniffs the sea
And rots and shivers here beneath St Mark.
Every house moves in Venice, drifting down
Canals of blackness to a mirrored town.

How easily we slip into abstraction,
And thoughts of gloom and distant things, things lost
Or never won, the sour fruits of inaction,
And joys that jaded with relentless cost.
Our very loves are ivied, fraction by fraction
Crumbling loose at the onset of frost.
– It isn't so, my sweet contessa, is it?
Ovid lodged *Tristia*, ours are but a visit.

And any time I feel myself go tristful,
I write a stanza to my staunch Teresa.
Knowing her short of patience for the wistful,
I improvise a shivaree to please her –
Throwing up a palace, fistful by fistful,
Of crystal, smarter than pyramids in Giza,
Within the Hyde Park of my mind. O Paxton,
Houser of catalogues undreamt by Caxton,

Such cornucopias of imperial trash –
Bronze Gothic chairs – three-hundred-bladed knives –
Pudic statues – rhino horns – calabash
And collapsible piano – sets of tropic gyves –
Such ludicrously philistine panache
As millions never saw in all their lives,
Or loved as soon as saw, or had displayed
Before them in a threadbare horsy glade.

Horses! God, I'm so fat. What a front to flaunt!
I rode my last horse fifteen years ago.
Today I'd float, not swim, the Hellespont.
And every winter this damned foot eats crow
(As Yankees say) and drags me taunt by taunt.
I'm just a sack of gibes, milord for show.
But dinna fash, lassie (as we Scots say).
We'll sing to keep the mulligrubs at bay.

We're at the nameless bottle now; it's good.
Your rings wink in the gaslight as you pour.
Gas is the thing; I never understood
Why some still rig their dripping candles galore,
Parlours like altars, wax-ends in the food.
Electric's next – science to the fore!
I think I'm ready for some bread and cheese.
Don't get up. I have the pantry keys.

There we are. Now if only Ada was here –
You know I miss my daughter – she can talk
Like an angel on sine and cosine, severe
But winning with it, you could never mock

40

The hypotenuse in her company, or sneer
Your way into some asymptotic baulk.
She's working all out now with Charles Babbage,
And that's a far cry from roast beef and cabbage.

It seems they have the plan for a machine
To do computing, a thousand sums a minute.
This engine has not trundled on the scene
Yet, but d'you think there might be something in it?
They need a language that is not – obscene –
Or human – or Albanian – or Inuit.
Ada wants the very machines to confer.
Perhaps they'll name the language after her.

Babbage and Marx – can that be what's to come?
Machines to compute, and all the workers free?
My dear contessa, what a maximum
Of bliss it would be to come back and see –
To burn the dungeons that have made men dumb,
And wade whole rivers to the liberty tree.
Burns said *I guess an' fear*. Ah when we do,
Mark then and shape the new life thundering through.

How red the fire is now – let it go down.
We never tried the pine-cones Lisa left us.
I must look out. The canal is silver-brown,
Half slurry and half sleet. Weather's bereft us
Of distant towers. Gondoliers would frown
But there are none. Whatever angel cleft us
Out of the rock is gone. We are ours to keep.
Bed, my love; pop the gas; to touch, and sleep.

Shakespeare: a Reconstruction

from Matthew Arnold, 'Shakespeare'

Others are open. You give a high smile
as you win the Prospero stakes, and silently
bury your books deeper than any auditor
could find them sound or unsound.
Did you 'die a papist', hate dogs, love swarthy
ironhaired women and fair flibbertigibbet men
or are the sonnets a load of. Cigarette foil
litters our searching and poring. You sit there
self-sustaining, a white cloud, while your wife
sews your new coat-of-arms *passim*. Better sew
than unpick! See Marlowe? Well.
All pains the immortal spirit must endure,
all weakness that impairs, all griefs that faze
rebels like him, you filched to salt your plays.

To the Queen: a Reconstruction

from Tennyson, 'To the Queen'

Revealed in death, will you still hold
Some nobler office upon earth
Than powdered arms or braided girth
Could give the wanton queens of old,

O Liberace? Royal grace
Floated you on a thousand stages
With the diamonds of the ages
And irresistible embrace

Stretched out for all, such love, such care,
Dracula in white mink, no time
To make demands of modern rhyme
With candelabra everywhere;

Now – where your honeyed music wakened
A million matrons' stifled calls,
And palace-like piano-walls
Vibrated as the yearning beckoned –

Take, Sir or Madam, this quick song;
For if your faults were thick as dust
In well-closed closets, you can't trust
The future will be kind. How long

Will those who thought you ruled your blood
Take to cross off your natal day,
And tell their children you were gay?
'She had her secrets since the Flood;

'She held court in another scene;
Her aides that saw her eyelids closed
Thought she could die undiagnosed,
But better far this wasted queen

43

'Should have a shroud of truth, and get
Its gritty ice on, not its mink
On shoulders, rings on hands – and shrink
From freedom as if narrower yet

'She had to go, in that decree
Which struck her throne and raked her till
Of tokens of the people's will,
And poled her Iron Maiden to sea.'

Chillon: a Reconstruction

from Byron, 'Sonnet on Chillon'

My God we must repel a plea for dungeons
even by the back door of mind over matter.
Anyone who says chained Biko's mind
was chainless underwrites tyranny.
Bonivard had it easy. A damp vault
six feet above lake-level? Dayless gloom
in 'really a spacious and rather airy vaulted room'?
Come on, I love you Byron, but that won't do.
What, Bunyan's Chillon was a holy place
because he begot his Pilgrim there?
That *Progress* never served progress!
Boethius left footprints too? *De Consolatione*
Philosophiae would suit Botha very neatly.
Let them appeal – it's quite safe – to God.

True Ease in Writing: a Reconstruction
from Pope, 'An Essay on Criticism', lines 362-73

True ease in writing comes to art by chance,
as those move easiest who break the dance
slightly, and almost imperceptibly –
but not quite – swing the senses surely, ably
out of the lock of echo, thud of sound,
even when classic numbers mow the ground
flat.
High maze hedges hide – but not quite – the hat
of the six-footer tangoing bravely through:
no, it does not take two.
And if sharp-fanged Carmilla scours the plain,
it is by moonlight, by fits and starts, for blood, with might and
    main.

On Time: a Reconstruction
from Milton, 'On Time'

I don't know about the snail, it's okay I think,
I don't envy it though. How could I,
having been to Lapland and back in a day,
stamping snowboots on Concorde steps
at tingling Rovaniemi with a New Year pack
of reindeer slices in my hand and
five hours of frozen river and pine
inside me, long or short
impossible to say.
Afterwards, that day seemed a week,
a fortnight, a world, Puck's world, a puck
birled across a void of sticks for luck.
Yet Concorde's a snail too,
I know it is. I'm number 102
in the civilian list for 1992's
space shuttle. Was, before the disaster. What year
will it be now? Like a supreme throne
high on time, the happy-making ship
half guides, half rocks me as I climb,
gross earth snail lapping broken glass,
never tired of stars, always longing to sit
in the brilliant cone, even with chance, even for a time.

Not Marble: a Reconstruction

from Shakespeare, Sonnet 55: 'Not marble...'

A Sqezy bottle in Tennessee,
if you want permanence, will press
a dozen jars into the wilderness.
It's bright, misspelt, unpronounceably
itself. No one loves you! I guess
there's *amour propre* in a detergent not to be
called sluttish. Vulgarity
dogs marble, gildings; monuments are a mess.
Exegi this, *exegi* that. Let's say
I am in love, crushed under the weight
of it or elated under the hush of it.
Let's not just say. I actually am.
Hordes, posterities, judges vainly cram
the space my love and I left yesterday.

Halley's Comet

I visit them from time to time, to see
their face and their state; seventy-six years
are in my sight but as a day. Old fears
have gone, they speed their little probes to me
but never guess that I might have a thought
to match. A ball of gritty slush, a tail
that whisks its gas about! They never fail
to measure what the measureless has brought,
and when it sails away from them they know
it must return. I have considered this,
and as I gulp their probes down I feel roused
and full of fire and eagerness to go
so far beyond them they will rage to miss
a torch so undemonstratively doused.

The Gorbals Mosque

Archbishops, moderators, and ambassadors,
high doctors and imams, administrators
and highest persons of goodwill joined hands,
delivered words, prayed, smoothed their bands
and threw their smiles to cameras; Egypt,
Mecca, Pakistan, Strathclyde, which outstripped
which in high amity by the minaret?
At dusk, the dome glowed like an amulet
among the gap-site detritus, the inaugurators
had swept back to their stations, the doors
leaked light. Sightseers lingered but not
for long, as mock-muezzins howled a shot
across their bows, and one boy with some wit
shouted 'White trash!' and his companion hit
a capping relish with 'Renegades!' while they strode
and laughed and kicked the rubble of the road,
raucously ululating into town,
but yet not really wishing the bright mosque down.

Rules for Dwarf-Throwing

1. If a dwarf is thrown through a glass window or glass door, he must wear gloves and a suitable mask.

2. If a dwarf is thrown through a burning hoop, extinguishers must be provided.

3. If a dwarf is thrown down a well, the organizers must ensure that the bottom of the well is dry, and is covered by leaves to a depth of three inches.

4. If a dwarf is to be thrown across the path of an oncoming train, the thrower must previously satisfy the organizers that he bears no personal malice to the throwee.

5. If a dwarf is thrown into a pond or river, he must wear a wetsuit and need not be tightly bound.

6. If dwarfs are thrown at night, they may be painted with phosphorescent paint, so that the point of impact may be clearly established.

7. If a dwarf refuses to be bound in the usual way before throwing, he may be put in a straitjacket of the requisite size.

8. If a dwarf utters any sound whatsoever, either in flight or at the moment of impact, the throw will be disqualified.

9. If a jockey impersonates a dwarf, and wins a competition because his light weight allows him to be thrown farthest, he will be liable to a fine of £1000 or three years imprisonment.

10. It is strictly forbidden, in dwarf-throwing literature and publicity, to refer to dwarfs as 'persons of restricted growth' or 'small people'.

The Bear

Come here, come here, I'm really playful today,
don't be afraid, they've even made me a chair
or a hammock of sorts I love to loll in
and surprise my visitors. I am never hungry
since I took this part. No no, I don't mean him,
Antigonus. Good lord, as soon as we're off stage
we jink a little sweet rough and tumble together
as like a dance as you ever saw, nothing
like death, nothing like death. I like that man.
He gives me herring from the brown barrel.
He gives me beer and honey once a week.
I could tear the lid right off that barrel
with a swipe and stuff myself stiff with fish
but I don't. I nuzzle the man. I get enough.
The only one I can't like is that Perdita,
she's a hussy in all that greenery-yallery,
with her pert stamping foot, his I should say,
these boys are a saucy pampered lot,
if they got some women I would really dance.
Antigonus though, he seems to like bears.
Strange man, but good. He won't change.
I love to creep up on him, hardly
breathing, stand at his back and tap
his shoulder. He never jumps,
just smiles. 'This is the chase,'
he says, 'we must go on for ever.'

Save the Whale Ball

(heading in *The Times*, 2 June 1981)

Is the Whale Ball worth saving? That is the real question.
What is to be said for and against it? Let us recall
the history and origin of the Whale Ball.
Old people – very old people – will perhaps remember
the Decade of Demise, when whale sightings thinned out
year by year, and the end could not be delayed.
Even whales pampered in oceanariums by every art
drooped and refused to mate. It was as if
some once promising species had beached
on a shelf of evolution they were not made to master.
So all that time their skeletons were gathered and stored,
in hundreds and in tens, and the last few. The world
agreed about them dead if not alive, no
whaling nation refused to subscribe to the monument.
Two generations of schoolchildren have yawned through
official films of the building of the Whale Ball,
but I have heard old men with sticks and bright eyes,
in sheltered housing and hospice, or sitting by the shore,
thrill to the memory of that idealism
and that propitiation, that overplus of patience and skill,
that overkill, that gigantic hyperborean scrimshaw
perched on a scarp at Angmagssalik.
How many dozen trainloads of whalebones were compacted
and fused into a spherical mass where the World
Trade Center and the Sydney Opera House could be inserted
like mites in a cheese, and how many craftsmen and sculptors
fretted the sphere into a thousand ancient scenes
of hunt and storm, with frozen seas and drowning men,
and flukes that smacked the arctic air, again, in bone, in vain,
in galleries of unfalling spray, and how that ball
as if some Chinese ivory ball had taken root and grown
rose white and huge into the mists of Greenland
and in a ceremony was declared fit and whole,
the records tell. Better than any barrow
of Beowulf or Breca, it broods like a boulder
from the beginning of time, and those who have heard

53

blizzards whistle their music through it
have come back half crazed with wonder.
But the Whale Ball is crumbling; it is too far north;
its cracks are widening, and its carved kayaks
have joined real kayaks in the sound. Some say
all megalomania has its reward: the dinosaurs,
the whales, the Whale Ball. Some would like nature
to regain the scattered bones, and in its ruthless welter
slowly rub off all signs of man, and roll
those rounded fragments in the deep-wombed currents
where who knows what might not be made of the dead.
Some would re-cast it in stainless steel; others
would pulverize it for talismans.
Some say we should have saved whales instead.

Dom Raja

If you cannot get your dead to burn,
if the wood will not take, and they are still there
accusing you mornings, evenings after,
if battering rain blurs the flame,
your work spent out in profitless smoke,
if your poverty cannot even steal
matches and oil, among the many waiting
to deliver ranks of other dead,
and flies seethe where fire should,
making the eyes move again and signal
they have an indomitable reproach
for you as you stand alive in the sun:
I will put an end to this if you call for me,
I promise I will make ashes if you need me,
I will leave your accuser without a tongue
if you can pay me, and if you believe
that I know the dead and their ways
and am their king.

I tell you they are not easy to destroy,
the dead. Sometimes with a rush they are back,
circling the camp relentlessly mourning
those that are dead to them, for you
are never as remorseless as they are,
they have no bread to bake or clothes
to wash or anything but time
to fill, and swarming through the bounds
they fall on you, they tear you, eat you,
spit you out to your terror as lacking
the substance they must have. The substance
they must have is not in you and can
never be, so why do they devour you?
I can tell you they are not unappeasable
if you will ask me to tell you. I could show you
how to harrow the little hell they march from
if you were good to me, a little.
You have only to take me aside
to see my kingdom.

Look how I have pushed the broken thing like an ark
burning straight down roaring to the water-line.
I dance, I am set on a throne, my torch
is never out. My suppliants put stones
on the bodies against jackals, and run
to search for me, they scuffle and pray
and ask me to melt their guilt to drops
of fat. The dead smell me far off.
I wrestle with them until they are black.
The Ganges reaches darkly seaward.
Look where I point: the smouldering riches
drift foul and slow, then rough and swift,
still fighting, still twisting towards the living,
still throwing indignations like anchors
to scrape and scour the frowning grief
that lines the banks. The dead are so restless
that even I have to drive them before me
with all my power, but if you want me to do so
– and how few there are who want me to do so –
I will keep them silent, weltering
at the feet of their king.

The Change

For all its banks bursting with bullion,
    the land of injustice will not prosper.

The skyscrapers shine as if they could never
    smell black smoke or shake to thunder.

Tanks, whips, dogs, laws – the panoply
    cracks steadily, being built over a fault.

Of course there are battleships, communications,
    planes; but the sophisticated do not have it.

The spirit has it, the spirit of the people has it,
    townships, shantytowns, jails, funerals

have it. It is no use digging in,
    rulers, unless you dig a pit to be

tipped into. Ruling has gone on too long,
    will not be saved by armbands or the laager.

The unjust know this very well.
    They lay ears to the ground, hear hooves.

Beasts, one time; an express, one time;
    men, one time; history, one time.

Straighten up and pat your holsters.
    Self-righteousness and a ramrod back

will not help. The sun goes down with you,
    other fruits ripen for other lips.

Vereshchagin's Barrow

With every war
Vereshchagin is trundled onto a dump of mammoths.
With every war
Goya is stuffed screaming into a geode.
With every war
Kollwitz lies buried in a terminal moraine.

'There in the permafrost you cannot
read, much of the night, or go south in the winter.
Thunder scurries over you faint as sparrows' feet,
cream-heavy fogs blunder and probe unseen,
blizzards howl no louder than feathergrass.
Lay the cold to your bones,
burrow in, past a few pressed shards and hooves,
you have hardly any dimension now, except time.
It is too late to try a sign, far less a cry.
You will never make that fossil tusk a horn
to rouse the dead or bring down walls
or even flute yourself to sleep –
fools without finger-tips,
lips drawn like packthread,
an arm crushed into a rib-case,
bellies full of peat.'

Goya stirs a thumbnail.
Vereshchagin stretches a toe.
Kollwitz twitches an eyelid.

'Why should you burrow upwards through the deadly soil?
Why should you want to break sorrow?
If ever you did burrow up, do you know, do you know
you would not meet air but a layer
of more permafrost impacted
in a desolate tumulus, a tangle
of Etendards and Harriers, Exocets and Sea-Darts,
Sea-Kings and Skyhawks, destroyers and destroyers?
Think about a mound
of drowned men and melted aluminium.

Can you fight your way through white-hot steel?
Can you paint the paint that's scorched off hulls?
Paint-flakes drift into snow-flakes.
The only flying-fish is the Exocet.
Car-crusher time has pushed it all on top of you.
We call it Vereshchagin's Barrow.'

    Vereshchagin groaned, kicked the mammoths' bones to
        ninepins.
    Kollwitz drove her brow like a prow through the glacier.
    Goya gave a shout, split the geode, flashed quartz.

'Well, I see there is no holding you.
Can you not take oblivion quietly?
What do wars end in but peace?
Do you think brush or pen or graver
can put flesh on a pyramid of skulls
or get a torso on a tree to sit at supper?
Are you still enslaved by Owen's old lie
that it is not sweet and fitting to die
for a homeland? Don't listen to us.
Nothing can tell you whether we are Furies
or Eumenides. Go off. Draw war.
If you have cameras, give them care.
In this world from which we speak to you
we do not trust artists any more.
I know, I know.
All right then, go.'

A mother gave her dead child's thumbprint to Kollwitz
without a word.
A hooded figure rose and followed Goya
without a word.
Sea-fogs trailed their coats for Vereshchagin
without a word.

Newspoems
(1965-1971)

The Newspoems were cut out from newspapers and other ephemeral material, pasted on to sheets of paper, and photographed. Most people have probably had the experience of scanning a newspaper page quickly and taking a message from it quite different from the intended one. I began looking deliberately for such hidden messages and picking out those that had some sort of arresting quality, preferably with the visual or typographical element itself a part of the 'point', though this was not always possible. What results is a series of 'inventions' both in the old sense of 'things found' and in the more usual sense of 'things devised'.

IF YOU'VE SEEN IT YOU HAVEN'T SEEN IT

1966

1968

safe
first,
whispered
man, as he tore
abel. If I didn't do
this it'd go before you could say
I keep it
sir.

1965

HALT
'COMMIT ADULTERY

1966

You can SING here

1966

want you blues

1968

Sick Man

Say

o

1968

Joe's Bar

**SORT OF PLACE YOU
SORT OF
YOU WISH**
until Midnight

1965

DONE!
CRANE FROM
CROW

1967

The new shape of o

1965

In Mid-Trepan

LOOK
there's

your head

-- it's just opened
because it's moving -- to
stay open while the

1967

In almost every
land there's a
green and silver bottle.
It holds an
electrifying liquid from
                    NOD
            bitterly cold.
            With bitter
            pleasure.
    NOD is the
icy jade. It tastes
        from the
            tower
        taking
        it.

1966

74

'I place
the
dead
ahead
of me,
and bong'

1971

I raised my hand and killed me.

1969

Mull is
a whale

1969

Chemical decides to liquidate

1969

OLD
FANS
UP
FOR FIRM
HOLD
PLAN
STAND

1969

PEOPLE
MADE TO
FEEL
PAW

1971

Apple Girl

A weeping
      icy and golden
   lass with the
     morning
  apples.
Sh
making love.

1969

**Wet your tongue with
a Pink
and discover
how dry it is.**
<small>the Pink!</small>

1966

"Literature
is news
that st
ews."

EZRA
POUND

1967

Why not be
    a Whole Cat?
Or a King, if you fancy
            a Handsome Prince?
Or an Ugly Oriental
        splendid choice in Nubile
            Villains
        of High-class Criminal
        Efficient
Distinguished
        Nick

1968

1969

RO
co
to
CO

1969

Pigeons: Elizabethan

What showr on's hat

1968

Meter eater

1970

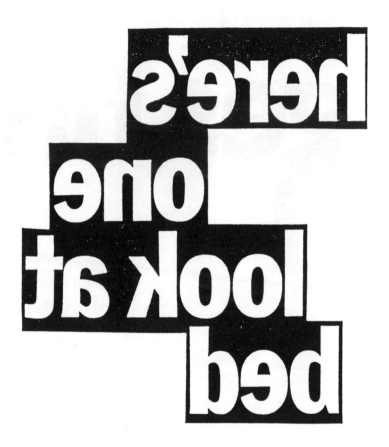

1966

ges ha
i

1969

Idyll

Toby D

arling

Ex

Red Cap

Wee Heavy

Nut Brown

Sweetheart

1965

I found
because
I couldn't
now
I can't
~~because~~
I found

1967

It is called

It does time

It is a total
software

It was
heaviest
processing—

Next it was
time sharing,
engineering
the same ease

You're looking at the real

crow. The

people are still in bed. The

figure behind the

hat's

him, a lark is

for people flying

from

those extra people who'll be

ready for even more than that.

Pass

beam

through the vast

Bird. He'll do

you.

Answer: DEATH

BALLA
D 13

Animal Loading
Harrows Mounted
Trailing, **Ballcove**
Ridgers, **Scarifiers**
Harrow Tines .

LIMIT

1965

not elegant, but
        broad rugby strip
            melancholy sludgy
                crocheted berets
                        winding
                            down

1965

Who is he?

He prefers his champagne
hand-tailored
companions beautiful
and his cigarettes

red

1966

Hypermarine

All
sails

on

1968

Ball

st
ot-
ting

1968

All
ons.
all
oot!

1967

GET
ИN
IT

1966

aire
is a
joy.

itself.
really
run.

1969

a testimonial
will think that you were
at your next convention.
will think your
invitation says
you're handsome.
tom
will think you've come from
your next club party and
you're going somewhere important
there in the nightclub and
you're a superb dancer, tennis
ride with a girl.
a liquor
all.
one will think you're
Monday morning.

1966

We made the decision reluctantly
after the first
to give   trouble. So people
with nice heart

are in business

So please, if you
go mad—

we're making them

1966

Little fish have to keep
time. The
king
knows all about
little fish.
We're only
rope.
There's no
emptying ashtrays
full before we rent
life.

1966

On their tenth anniversary
will expire. But the knives
                  will smile,
they were
married. And they'll

              marvel
what about us?

1966

Il a toujours quelque chose

Dernièrement

Il fume

à s'en plaindre. Oh, rien

d'ailleurs il parle

Je lui ai

Il ne s'est pas tû

il n'arrête pas

leur goût

Bref, il ne jure plus

Mais il a encore

de grogner :

Tu ne pouvais pas

1966

Starting today, we're putting our
machine in the place.
Hands in the business
by their red gloves.
It's not that
we're as automated
but that we
don't. Machines don't
at all.
Which is all right
all right.

1968

Concrete Ballad of Reading Gaol

ome

o

he

o

1965

Visual Soundpoem

go

1967

Found Concrete Poem: The Enactment

S
UTURE

1969

1968

From the Video Box
(1986)

ad te, ut video, comminus accessit
Cicero, *Letters to Atticus*

From the Video Box

1

I saw that Burning of the Books, in China
I don't know how many centuries B.C.
If anything was compulsive on the set,
that was. You could almost feel the heat,
and when you saw the soldiers and flunkeys dancing
like demons against the glare, bending and lifting,
lifting and throwing, throwing and grimacing through the sparks,
and when you heard the crackle and spit of the wood
going off like fireworks, and they had fireworks too,
or I think they had, it was hard to be sure,
but anyway the bonfires getting bigger and bigger
and those gongs looming and booming in the smoke,
when you'd seen and heard all that,
I thought it was the best the old classics
had ever done for them, to warm a few hands
in a freezing night like that: there were no long faces,
I noticed, and no one ran with tongs
to snatch a few analects out of the flames.
This was first-class entertainment.
That emperor had the right idea.
That's really all I wanted to say.

2

I have just watched that fearful programme
of the burning of the Library at Alexandria.
I rushed to the box – I am still shaking –
to record my disgust that any producer
should foist such barbarous philistinism –
without introduction, without discussion –
on a million homes. Accident, arson, act of war –
I don't care what the miserable excuse is
for showing the death of books, live, on screen.
Men, I could understand; but books! –
all right, call them rolls, scrolls, codexes –

115

not one, not ten, oh no, but tens of thousands,
irreplaceable, perishable, unprinted, unique!
That was the grandeur that was Rome did that.
Then they had the nerve to show us an epilogue
when anything that was left six centuries later
was burned by the Arabs as pagan trash.
I shall certainly write straight to the Authority.
There are limits to what an ordinary man
can stomach, or should stomach. I admit my wife
was not worried, but then not everyone is a reader;
I'm sure she supports me though. Well I think that's it.

3

This is the first time I have ever recorded
my reaction, and I speak with some diffidence,
but surely the display of that conflagration
which laid the new British Library in ashes
must rate as quite unusually riveting.
The interest is greater in that every device
known to technology, heat detectors,
sprinkler systems, flameproof furniture,
fire doors, foam-capsuled mosaic floors
proved powerless to stop the hungry spread.
I thought to begin with it must be *son et lumière*
on the grand scale, but then the whole building
glowed bright orange through the firegrate of itself
and sent fireflies up into the north London night
that were soon to be charred falling flakes
of bindings, catalogues, incunabula.
The popping of the terminals, the melting of the fiches
presented future film-makers, I guess,
with such a lurid viable store of image and sound
I could see the library burning and toppling again and again.
On the old Bloomsbury site there was never
a spectacle as all-enfolding as this.
Silent now the dead tongue in 11375.cc.13!

Scandals of Cup.1000.c.7. all at rest!
And 12452.w.3. quavering in his sprightly grave!
Whoever was responsible for this show
was a person of imagination, and bold almost to excess.

4

I never believed in legendary heroes
till I saw that scratch video of Tantalus
video of Tantalus how could they get it
it was no actor no actor there he was
tall and muscular severe very swarthy and sad
naked but for shining leather sandals
shining leather sandals and a bronze fillet
round his black his black hair it was the way
he ran through the dust storm parched panting
it was the way he ran into that bright fresh river
fresh river to plunge and slake but the water
sucked itself back so that he could not reach it
stretched up through the heady air parched panting
to the overhanging orange-trees that jerked away
orange-trees jerked away it was the way
he suffered hope deferred jerked away
oh I know we were told he had stolen
Zeus's cupbearer to wait at his own table
and more but it was the way he stood
way he stood in that ruthless stream
that made me shiver and so feel for him
when the image of Ganymede flashed through the spray
for it he was allowed to touch it it was a shade
if it was real he was not allowed to touch it
if it was a shade he was allowed to touch it
if he was not allowed to touch it it was real
it was the way he ran it was the way
he stood severe very swarthy and sad

5

I am not here to talk about a scratch
video I am here to make a scratch I am
here to make a scratch video to make
tape-recorder on *a young man of mysterious*
appearance coming towards me fore-edge
painting flip a friend did this flip of me
jumping flip from bank to flip bank
like the force of enchantment miniature home video
watch it miniature home video I am bounding
into fields and woods back back I am
bounding from the door towards the fields
I am moving towards the door a friend
took this *I was now a justified person*
watch this close-up in the woods I fan
a batch of polaroids like a fore-edge painting
I fan a batch of swimming to the farther bank
and rising shaking water everywhere
the clothes were the same to the smallest item
and my clothes are still damp as you can see
my clothes are still damp with I think a
think a hint of steam in this hot video box
this singular being read my thoughts in my looks
I have nothing more to show the camera
anticipating the very words that I was going to utter
to show the camera after I have let
you see my friend who has been
behind me all this time
all this time and here he is
beside me now here we are
thank you thank you

6

my friend and I watched that scratch that scratch video
last night we watched that last night I was
on the black chesterfield and Steve was on the
black chair not that that will interest viewers

interest viewers but I want to be authentic
on the black the black chesterfield just as the sun
went down reddish outside and I could switch
from the set to the sky and back sky and back
and back back there was a squeezed sunset
on the set between gables and a helicopter cut
through the reddish screen like a black tin-opener
while suddenly a crow flew suddenly a crow
a crow flew through the real red outside what we
call the real red and tore it silently it silently
a scratch in air never to be solved scratch
in air Steve said never solved as inside
back went the helicopter to start again
to start again I said those gables don't
grow dark those gables don't grow dark
that's what I want to say they don't grow
dark those gables on the set

7

It is hard to know what it is I saw.
I had been switching through a score of channels
in that disgruntled and half-idle mood I'm sure you know,
a gloomy winter's evening with the curtains open,
the streetlamps on and the cars racing home,
and gusts of wind that shook the house,
raced off with armfuls of showers to the river.
Who can be happy? Not I. But the search
goes on, even through that flurry of switched images,
as if a picture, if at least it moved, could move
the sluggish heart. Everything happens, perhaps.
There was suddenly something growing on the screen
that could kick-start hope racing forward
into I don't know what roads of years.
There were no images, that's the hardest part.
The whole screen was a swirling dirty grey
that churned and churned and held the attention
only to wonder what it was; but there in the middle

it seemed to split like a skin, a thin
horizontal streak of blue flashed out –
no, it did not flash, that was only the surprise
of the contrast, it was too pure a blue,
an eggshell blue, a sky blue, blue
of an innocent eye, not harsh or icy,
not brooding dark or royal,
not feeble pastel either,
but clear and steady, beautiful and true.
It grew, like a rift in the clouds after rain,
or like the slow opening of an eye,
until the grey clouds, the grey lids, gathered
their hideous strength and grain by grain
joined seamlessly together once again.
Wherever I go I see that patch of blue.
Did anyone else watch it? Is there happiness?
Hope in things that come and go?
Why should we not know?

8

This is the most ridiculous thing I ever experienced
and I hope whoever is listening will take note.
I am not paying good money for such stupidities.
There is something wrong with Channel 49.
I was settling down last night for that old film,
I tell you I was just settling back with a sandwich
and a can of lager when the screen went pink,
then rosy, then red, absolutely red,
no announcement, no music, no captions, no anything.
It was very late. It was very quiet. The family
were in bed long ago. Here I am
waiting for my all-night movie and the set,
I almost said the bloody set, goes red.
I shook it, switched off, on; still red.
Well, I sat and watched it! What would you have done?
It got deeper, darker, seemed to glisten.
I crushed the empty can, got up and threw it
in the kitchen bin, came back,
touched the set on an impulse,

pressed the screen or stroked it,
I don't remember, only an impulse,
and stared at my hand, it was wet
and sticky and red as blood or red with blood,
who knows, what sort of programme was that
and who lets these things happen?
Look, I didn't wipe it off. See that, camera.
You think I'm crazy? Think again.
I know we get our mail through the set, bills,
bank balances, but blood is ridiculous.
I want a clean dry screen from now on.
Let them bleed elsewhere, whoever they are.

9

At last, a programme for the colour-blind!
Here we come, tail-end of so many minorities
but never mind: congratulations all round.
It was a stroke of genius to use Kerouac's friend,
that red-green colour-blind wild Neal Cassady
who worked on the railroad and drove a train
through as many signals as would have crashed
the push of a less charmed supercharger.
We saw how he cheated at the Ishihara,
got the job to show man can do anything.
Well, that's all right. I don't admire him
to distraction, but I do admire
the secret film he made
for his fellow colour-blinders. All you out there
with your green green grass and your red red rose
saw your conventional story,
a bar, a shoot-out, a car-chase,
as my friends tell me,
but we saw something different,
oh, very different, and it is something you will never know
unless we tell you, because you cannot see it –
it is the same film, but strain as you will,
your lovely normal eyes will never figure
that carpet, our carpet,
rolled out from its orient.

10

I never really took to Shakespeare
until I saw that extract of the death
of Ragozine. We were not told
what play it was. The cell he lay in
was windowless and would have been black
but the half-kind jailers had left him a candle
because of his sickness. I thought the way
the fever made him toss and turn so much
that the candle-flame was never still
and threw a twisted shadow-play of his misery
on the old rough dripping graffiti'd walls
was a good touch. Everything flickered
like an ancient film, while his sweat seeped
into the paillasse: pirate's malaria
shook him, racked him worse than any rack,
hallucinated him till he shouted
he had brought a whole bastard boarded golden
Turkish argosy back limping to Ragusa
and could count his coins for life –
the bey was trussed, the scimitars were piled,
the bey was piled, the scimitars were trussed,
and he was the pirate of the western world –
oh I liked that. And the last moment
when his chest heaved right up, and his hand tried to,
his right hand, for the left one had been shot,
and his one gold earring flashed in the candlelight,
and he cried out in what was more defiance
than desperation before he slumped back dead,
I thought the entire prison must have shivered
as I did. But no, nothing so obvious.
Soon there was that sturdy singing executioner
rattling the bars with his axe and roaring,
I want a head! Where is that villain? I need his head! –
strode in, tore off the earring, struck.
And the staring head was stuffed in a bag,
swinging off as the credits rolled.
If that was Shakespeare, he's my man.

11

Poor Barbary! I must tell you
I switched off. I knew she was going to die.
I mustn't blame the programme-makers
but I saw myself there as she pined away.
It was a good scullery, quite bright,
where she scoured the pots, but nothing could hide
her sharp high shoulders and pinched cheeks,
she was almost a shadow as she hung up her cloth
and stared out listlessly at the canal.
When she took a chair
to sew and mend, nearer the window,
she could hardly drag it, or the basket
filled with her good mistress's stockings and kerchiefs.
She had stopped eating altogether since her lover went mad,
carted off to Bedlam. I have stopped eating altogether
since my lover jilted me for the army. It seems the same.
Scour pots; sew; faint; be put in sheets; end it.
Shakespeare knew when some can live
without the other and some have not the luck to.
Her song was terrible
when she laid the needle aside,
sing all a green willow,
her hair falling down like the willow
towards the flags of the floor.
I could take no more.
I cannot ask anyone
except the millions
out there, you,
what I have to do.

12

Oh the sheer power of that witch, that bitch, that
bit and talon of what universe, that Sycorax!
I had to come and say I love it when
there's no morality left, not a chink or a cheep
from damned good or damned evil we keep

hearing about, nothing but a screen
brimmed up with pure force and nothing lagging
in the energy not a stint in the energy
it pushes into our veins like acid.
I watched all those Shakespeare scenes, but this
beat the sentiment straight out of the rug, hung it up
like a felucca's grandmother, winds and tempests
could only batter it better and better. What a beast
she was as she scoured the brush of the island,
bent like a hoop but pregnant too, her eyelids
fuel-blue, her mouth crushed red with berries,
arms all whipcords, straining at last
like a wombed Samson between two pines.
She never brought the sky down but she brought
thúnder down without a groan as she straddled
her slippery man-child brought down
wawling in a squall and squelch
of monsoon rain. She reigns,
bitch-queen, batch-quern, grinds out
pure nature, calves icebergs, makes archipelagos,
and I saw her suddenly in a final shot
solid with her thighs about the world,
frowning at a thousand twangling instruments
that to her were neither here nor there.
How good it is to have a set for that one!

13

I don't watch television,
but I was passing the box
and I would just like to say
if anyone is interested
that I really think
John MacLean is the greatest.
The Nationalists will never
win without Labour,
and Labour is useless
sitting in London.

They've all sold politics
for a mess of pottage
called economics.
They want more jobs
and that's all right,
but they never say republic
and that's all wrong.
My father told me –
and he knew MacLean –
'If people look at you
when you swear by the bones
of Baird and Hardie,
don't explain,
but don't forget.'
Neither I do.
It's as simple as that.
But somebody has to say it.
Well, I must move on.
Your box is quite nice.
Remember what I said.

14

Wait noo, wait a minute. Right.
Howzzat, eh? Big yin, innit?
See when it gets hard, thir a bend in it.
Yeah. Wait. Therr ye go. Yeah. Weird.
Lassies never complain but.
Hope yir camera's good at close-ups? Therr noo.
Well, that's yir loat. I'll away.
Ma mates are waitin. Wave
goodbye, Willie. Right,
in ye go. Yeah. Christ
it's a tight fit in thae jeans.
Never mind, that's me wan a tenner.
Auf wiedersehen, pets.

15

I know you won't mind if I use your box
for a *cri de coeur*. My, cat, has, gone,
vanished without a trace, I have not seen him
for a week, and I am *quite distracted*.
He is a marmalade cat called Robertson,
he is big and beautiful and an absolute *bumper*
of a creature, you could not miss him,
he is *sui generis* and *sine qua non*.
There *is* a tiny tiny tiny nick
in his left ear which I would *not* mention
but for the identification; he is *all cat*.
And he should be wearing a
smart smooth polished dark brown real leather collar
which was *so* carefully chosen
to go with that *lovely* lovely fluffy warm gold fur,
and his name and address are on it.
To those who are watching – I don't say he's been *abducted*,
it's just he has such a trusting trusting nature,
he would go with anyone for a kind word,
or a *little* fillet sole, he does not *gobble* or snatch,
and he purrs at your legs like a *percolator*.
Well what more can I say,
Robertson is a treasure, a dear, a *rara avis*, a gift –

and if any of you have him I want him back *pronto*.

16

There may be a case for subliminal images
but whatever backroom mandarin thought it could be made
by showing, or rather not showing, the Big Bang
was off his cosmic top. Technical triumph
I grant you, if we are to believe the programme-makers,
since there they were plugged into the very beginning,
the very first stir and flutter, the evulsion of nothing,
instead of their usual toytown graphics. They told us
we must watch out for it, the programme would not help.

There was only one window, one moment they could use.
It was some messy story about the Borgias,
all tiger-striped galleries with grille-filtered light,
and lean figures darting among pillars, and silks
hissing suddenly with skirts gathered up;
and pictures, bronzes, fountains, altars, footmen,
girls with cushions, boys with greyhounds,
dwarfs with pisspots, shrieks from birdcages,
great bangs from studded doors crashed shut
were flung about the screen
like counters in a game.
There was never a second when nothing was happening.
If you were not quick you missed the nod,
the heel-scrape, the thumb-twitch, the slipped veil,
you saw the doused torch, not the glow of the phial.
I reckon it was ninety per cent subliminal,
so why add more? I saw nothing,
my friends saw nothing. Just once perhaps,
in the banquet scene, when the servant
set down a purple pitcher of wine
which turned out to be the only one not poisoned,
and the camera looked straight down into the wine
to make us think it really had been poisoned –
it was that sort of film – I thought I saw a tremor
on the dark surface that was not caused
by the careful placing of the vessel on the table.
I recorded it, and played it again.
I said I recorded it, and played it again.
I played it slowly, and I played it again.
Well, there was nothing. It seems the duke
had gently banged the table for his chaplain
(one of the chief villains) to say grace.
Mind you, the nature of things is so sly
that the two tremors could be timed as one.
Be that as it may, and thank you very much,
but I am still waiting for the universe to begin.

17

That was so strange last night –
I thought I saw my son
who was lost overboard in a storm
off Valparaiso – five years gone –
I know he was drowned, his body
was washed up on the rocks
and brought back home to Gourock
where I can see his grave.
There are no ghosts. What I saw
in that split-second flash
was an image only a mother
could be sure to be her son,
to have been her son surely
since he was no longer there.
It came in a blizzard of images,
a speeded mosaic of change
in the Americas, I watched
half bored, irritated
by the strident music, ready
to switch channels – then!
– not in his seaman's cloth
but a camouflage jacket,
looking straight at the camera,
his fist in a revolutionary salute,
a letter sticking from his pocket
with writing I saw as mine.
Oh how little we know
of those we love! Perhaps
it was sabotage, not storm,
that sank his ship – perhaps
that broken body after all
was not – oh images, images,
corners of the world seen
out of the corner of an eye –
subversive, subliminal –
where have you taken my son
into your terrible machine
and why have you peeled off

my grief like a decal
and left me a nobody
staring out to sea?

18

There is one word
that should never be seen
except when you think you may have seen it
but are not sure.
It should never be lingered over or built up
or allowed to hang heavy and ornate
and should only be like lightning in summer,
the next thing to an absence.
No bustling presence
can move men, the sun, the stars –

There is one message
you must not spell out,
but let it slip like a smolt
beween weeds and vanish,
or like a quicksilver lizard
freeze on the rock.
Give it between shots
if you will, if you may, if you can. And yet
remember there is nothing rosicrucian about it,
it is not for adepts,
it gives everyone joy
in the flick of a tail,
the flicker of a tongue –

Neither noun nor verb
rules; what is
needs what does.
Let it in and let it go – so
quickly – programme-makers,
seed-sowers in the burning screen!

I was galloping down through Patagonia
on a breakneck nag a fortnight back,
prospecting a bit, rumbling the sierras,
paddling and pottering in some salty lagunas,
keeping a swarm of baas at bay
and wishing I could shear the mineral fleece
from the humpbacks and the crags –
well all that's by the way, but not entirely.
Clattering east along a dried-up watercourse,
I switched on my wristwatch television
(and I should add that these jewelled creatures
are my delight, as they are today to so many)
and caught in its amazing unflickering clarity
an astronaut probing some Martian rille –
I groaned as he twirled up his subsoil sample
of red-veined if not red-blooded riches –
and the fool's clear voice came over saying
'Once water, always water' – he was searching for life!
Good God, we've got life galore –
twenty million sheep in Patagonia –
while the mountains are sleeping on nations' ransoms.
I could take the pick from my saddle-bag and
strike not water from the rock like idiot Moses
but rock, and rock again, and coal, and silver, and shale,
and whistle down to the coastal corridor
my little tuneless clinking hoofbeaten song
of mineralogy and materiality.
Pusillanimous Mars-prodders I can switch off,
did switch off. But such a fine coincidence
I had to tell you about. I was reinforced.
I had it all on my wrist like a gulf-man's hawk
and I sent it off right back to Mars.
The picture winked, as well it might.
I sold my horse, boarded a flight
from Comodoro Rivadavia,
and here I am. Bless TV, bless video.
You think I don't mean it but I do.
Did you ever have my type in your box?

'Video wall, video wall,
which is the fairest of them all?'
I am sure the great video wall debate
will not be resolved by my participation,
but here is what I think: there are walls
and walls, and a wallful of videos seen
on the small screen is virtually de-walled
and pretty pithless, even if it is pretty.
Leave it for connoisseurs of the pretty,
paperweight-fanciers, home-birds, page-turners, chintz-persons.
I want wall video to be all wall.
I want to be there and to feel wall-ness.
And I don't mean a straight flat look-this-way wall either,
with me in the middle, three metres back, staring,
lacking nothing but a Victorian neck-clamp.
No, I need a total mobile wraparound,
a dome of many-coloured glass, in fact,
that will not only stain the white radiance
of any eternity there may be but
oh, oh,
positively dance round the
threescore, fivescore wedded, embedded
screens of talk, tale, trail, and trial.
You think it's over the top? A touch of Sardanapalus?
'Everyone knows a plain background's best for pictures.'
Not a bit of it!
Try my wall,
climb into my shell,
sell your house, bring your family,
sharpen your eyes and your wits until
the dance is story and the story dance,
and as you run forward you feel time run forward
to fetch the age of gold. Oh
you would never be ill or old
if I could build my hall, my video wall,
no, never at all.

Against my will, and I emphasize that,
I bought one of those portable chameleon televisions
which were going to revolutionize viewing.
Revolutionize my epidiascope!
You take the thing into a field of cows –
you've got the news read in a field of cows.
You take it skin-diving – oh yes it's waterproof, it's everything –
and the string quartet saws through giant kelp.
I had mine in Glencoe – there was a film about Glencoe –
it disappeared.
The brochure spoke of
'melting the boundaries between art and reality',
'hilarious or sinister juxtapositions',
'a set that can never bore'.
I have put it next to the microwave
in the hope of precipitating an identity-crisis
and if it results in mutual self-destruction
it will be worth it.
It really is time I went back to find out.

22

I put up the biggest dish in Perthshire
and all I got was ВРЕМЯ, ВРЕМЯ, ВРЕМЯ.
I do exaggerate, of course. I also had
a brief harangue from Tripoli, from a tent if you please,
all swags and carpets and bits of brass –
had to argue closely with my wife
who thought the man was charming.
How can you say he is charming, I asked her,
when you don't understand a word of Arabic?
It's his eyes, she said. What can you do?
Language is the devil. We keep hearing
about the wonders of science, and satellite TV
will 'bring the world into our living-room',
but these chaps in Moscow will not speak English,
I can't think why, since it's the best language,

but they won't. So where are the translation-machines
up in the satellites, why can't we hear
all those little Japanese beavers using
the language Shakespeare wrote and Churchill spoke?
That's my first complaint.
The second is interference.
I had painfully managed to home in
on a splendid meeting of those new men
of the right in Paris, and was beginning to follow
something of what they said, from words like 'France'
and 'pays' and 'tradition' and 'responsabilité',
when suddenly everything dissolved in a welter
of crocodiles threshing through some muddy shallows
while tribesmen shouted and beat drums.
It was sickening.
In Perthshire we like a job well done.
If there are teething troubles, get working.
If I need a larger dish, tell me.
If your satellite is foreign-made – I shall find out.

23

It is grand and fine to think
how the satellites in their places
are waiting to receive and give
it all. What shall we live to see?
White dish, listening eye:
if objects can be poetry,
you are. When you filled my screen
with a slow swoop over the masts
of America's Very Large Array
I thought between you you might bring
non-existent neumes and breves
from the long-exploded spheres.
You know my friends are hard on me,
they say it's a sin to be naive
and not a sign of innocence.
When did you last see a star suffering,

they ask me, or a dish writing,
or a V.L.A. making deserts bloom?
Why bounce trash from a great height?
Soaps are soaps even in Greek.
What is *Agamemnon* but a soap,
I try to reply. They miss the point.
Yes I've seen rubbish – violent
American rubbish, high-minded French
rubbish, hysterical Italian rubbish,
dignified Russian rubbish, silly
English rubbish, smiling Chinese
rubbish, maudlin Scottish rubbish –
but don't tell me I haven't seen
the dearest listeningest large array
where Adam covers half Iraq
and Eve in clouds bends over him,
and they are like a group, with stars.
What channel was that? The raucous laugh
rings round the yard: a hollow sound
to me. Think about it, viewers.
I shall go back, climb into my dish
and curl up like an oyster there,
swept by tides from everywhere.

24

Hullo there. That's my hamster, by the way,
in my breast-pocket, not my handkerchief.
He's the tamest creature you saw in your born days,
loves cameras too, so don't be alarmed.
What I came to say was
I won a satellite dish in a competition
which so far is a dead loss.
I tuned to a whaling epic from California,
but whenever a whale was harpooned
it turned into a baby, and some hydrophone
magnified the screams: they nearly split the house;
the blood was gallons, whale's blood, boiling out

till you got a puckered shrunken thing like a punctured doll.
Then the ship rocked in huge pressure waves,
and the set shook too; it did.
Now if I want protest I'll ask for it.
If I want excitement I want excitement.
See my hamster:
anyone that tries to harpoon him
gets a Stanley knife in his guts.
You can see from the look of me I mean that.
Well, you can see the knife too: there.
All I'm saying is
I hate arty-farty stuff,
and if that's the best you can do
I'll take down the dish and make
a swimming-pool for the hamster.
I like things straight. That's about it. All right?

25

If you ask what my favourite programme is
it has to be that strange world jigsaw final.
After the winner had defeated all his rivals
with harder and harder jigsaws, he had to prove his mettle
by completing one last absolute mindcrusher
on his own, under the cameras, in less than a week.
We saw, but he did not, what the picture would be:
the mid-Atlantic, photographed from a plane,
as featureless a stretch as could be found,
no weeds, no flotsam, no birds, no oil, no ships,
the surface neither stormy nor calm, but ordinary,
a light wind on a slowly rolling swell.
Hand-cut by a fiendish jigger to simulate,
but not to have, identical beaks and bays,
it seemed impossible; but the candidate –
he said he was a stateless person, called himself Smith –
was impressive: small, dark, nimble, self-contained.
The thousands of little grey tortoises were scattered
on the floor of the studio; we saw the clock; he started.

His food was brought to him, but he hardly ate.
He had a bed, with the light only dimmed to a weird blue,
never out. By the first day he had established
the edges, saw the picture was three metres long
and appeared to represent (dear God!) the sea.
Well, it was a man's life, and the silence
(broken only by sighs, click of wood, plop of coffee
in paper cups) that kept me fascinated.
Even when one hand was picking the edge-pieces
I noticed his other hand was massing sets
of distinguishing ripples or darker cross-hatching or
incipient wave-crests; his mind,
if not his face, worked like a sea.
It was when he suddenly rose from his bed
at two, on the third night, went straight over
to one piece and slotted it into a growing central patch,
then back to bed, that I knew he would make it.
On the sixth day he looked haggard and slow,
with perhaps a hundred pieces left,
of the most dreary unmarked lifeless grey.
The camera showed the clock more frequently.
He roused himself, and in a quickening burst
of activity, with many false starts, began
to press that inhuman insolent remnant together.
He did it, on the evening of the sixth day.
People streamed onto the set. Bands played.
That was fine. But what I liked best
was the last shot of the completed sea,
filling the screen; then the saw-lines disappeared,
till almost imperceptibly the surface moved
and it was again the real Atlantic, glad
to distraction to be released, raised
above itself in growing gusts, allowed
to roar as rain drove down and darkened,
allowed to blot, for a moment, the orderer's hand.

26

What was the best programme?
Oh, it was Giotto's O.
I don't argue the case
that it really was the past,
tapped under conditions
made suddenly favourable.
But how could any actor
so unpreparedly, so
swiftly yet so surely and
so gloriously seize
a sheet of pure white paper
and with black loaded brush
paint a perfect circle?
The camera was so close
that no trick or device
could have stayed undetected.
No, it was Giotto's O.
The papal envoy, I observed,
crossed himself at the sight –
needlessly, there was no magic
either black or white, it
was only the life of a man
concentrated down
to his finger-tips in the great
final ease of creation
which in its silence and
no longer laboriously
circles round and out.

27

The programme that stays most in my mind
was one you called the Dance of the Letters.
The graphics here was altogether
crisp and bright and strong and real.
First that gallows, with the dust
whirling across the square to sting

a blackened and unfeeling face
and tear at the unreadable placard
pinned to its slowly twisting chest
resolved itself into a T.
Then the car, in bird's-eye view,
crawling through narrow streets to bang
its bomb-load and its girl martyr
into a crowded market-place
stopped, became a fiery H.
Mothers, children, grandfathers, all
knew how to line the desert dirt-road
in a few black rags, and stretch out bowls
in their twig arms or hold out only
arms, till their appeal froze
in stifling fly-black heat to form
an E. But then another E
was gently, tentatively drawn
from the hard, half-shining prongs
of a rake; the gnarled gardener
was keeping his patch clean and rich,
weedless and airy, able to deliver
the vegetables of the year.
In a courtyard, shaded with awnings,
where a tethered, slew-mouthed camel chewed,
one red earthen water-jar
as old as history waited in its stand,
turning at last into an N.
A fisherwoman, pregnant, walked
slowly along a rocky shore,
but then transformed into a ship
with blowing spinnaker sailed out
in her whole woman's life to break
silence only with the whipping
of the sheets and with the song
she or the wind threw back to us.
She left us, melted into the white
of a D that rang out through the blue.

Sonnets from Scotland
(1984)

O Wechsel der Zeiten! Du Hoffnung des Volks!
Brecht

Slate

There is no beginning. We saw Lewis
laid down, when there was not much but thunder
and volcanic fires; watched long seas plunder
faults; laughed as Staffa cooled. Drumlins blue as
bruises were grated off like nutmegs; bens,
and a great glen, gave a rough back we like
to think the ages must streak, surely strike,
seldom stroke, but raised and shaken, with tens
of thousands of rains, blizzards, sea-poundings
shouldered off into night and memory.
Memory of men! That was to come. Great
in their empty hunger these surroundings
threw walls to the sky, the sorry glory
of a rainbow. Their heels kicked flint, chalk, slate.

Carboniferous
For I.R.

Diving in the warm seas around Bearsden,
cased in our superchitin scuba-gear,
we found a world so wonderfully clear
it seemed a heaven given there and then.
Hardly! *Et in Arcadia*, said the shark,
ego. We stumbled on a nest of them.
How could bright water that hid nothing stem
our ancient shudder? They themselves were dark,
but all we saw was the unsinister
ferocious tenderness of mating shapes,
a raking love that scoured their skin to shreds.
We feared instead the force that could inter
such life and joy, in fossil clays, for apes
and men to haul into their teeming heads.

141

Post-Glacial

The glaciers melt slowly in the sun.
The ice groans as it shrinks back to the pole.
Loud splits and cracks send shudders through the shoal
of herring struggling northwards, but they run
steadily on into the unknown roads
and the whole stream of life runs with them. Brown
islands hump up in the white of land, down
in the valleys a fresh drained greenness loads
fields like a world first seen, and when mild rains
drive back the blizzards, a new world it is
of grain that thrusts its frenzied spikes, and trees
whose roots race under the stamped-out remains
of nomad Grampian fires. Immensities
are mind, not ice, as the bright straths unfreeze.

In Argyll

For A.R.

We found the poet's skull on the machair.
It must have bobbed ashore from that shipwreck
where the winged men went down in rolling dreck
of icebound webs, oars, oaths, armour, blind air.
It watches westward still; dry, white as chalk,
perfect at last, in silence and at rest.
Far off, he sang of Nineveh the blest,
incised his tablets, stalked the dhow-bright dock.
Now he needs neither claws nor tongue to tell
of things undying. Hebridean light
fills the translucent bone-domes. Nothing brings
the savage brain back to its empty shell,
distracted by the shouts, the reefs, the night,
fighting sleet to fix the tilt of its wings.

The Ring of Brodgar

'If those stones could speak —' Do not wish too loud.
They can, they do, they will. No voice is lost.
Your meanest guilts are bonded in like frost.
Your fearsome sweat will rise and leave its shroud.
I well recall the timeprint of the Ring
of Brodgar we discovered, white with dust
in twenty-second-century distrust
of truth, but dustable, with truths to bring
into the freer ages, as it did.
A thin groan fought the wind that tugged the stones.
It filled an auditorium with pain.
Long was the sacrifice. Pity ran, hid.
Once they heard the splintering of the bones
they switched the playback off, in vain, in vain.

Silva Caledonia

The darkness deepens, and the woods are long.
We shall never see any stars. We thought
we heard a horn a while back, faintly brought
through barks and howls, the nearest to a song
you ever heard in these grey dripping glens.
But if there were hunters, we saw not one.
Are there bears? Mist. Wolves? Peat. Is there a sun?
Where are the eyes that should peer from those dens?
Marsh-lights, yes, mushroom-banks, leaf-mould, rank ferns,
and up above, a sense of wings, of flight,
of clattering, of calls through fog. Yet men,
going about invisible concerns,
are here, and our immoderate delight
waits to see them, and hear them speak, again.

Pilate at Fortingall

A Latin harsh with Aramaicisms
poured from his lips incessantly; it made
no sense, for surely he was mad. The glade
of birches shamed his rags, in paroxysms
he stumbled, toga'd, furred, blear, brittle, grey.
They told us he sat here beneath the yew
even in downpours; ate dog-scraps. Crows flew
from prehistoric stone to stone all day.
'See him now.' He crawled to the cattle-trough
at dusk, jumbled the water till it sloshed
and spilled into the hoof-mush in blue strands,
slapped with useless despair each sodden cuff,
and washed his hands, and watched his hands, and washed
his hands, and watched his hands, and washed his hands.

The Mirror

There is a mirror only we can see.
It hangs in time and not in space. The day
goes down in it without ember or ray
and the newborn climb through it to be free.
The multitudes of the world cannot know
they are reflected there; like glass they lie
in glass, shadows in shade, they could not cry
in airless wastes but that is where they go.
We cloud it, but it pulses like a gem,
it must have caught a range of energies
from the dead. We breathe again; nothing shows.
Back in space, *ubi solitudinem*
faciunt pacem appellant. Ages
drum-tap the flattened homes and slaughtered rows.

144

The Picts

Names as from outer space, names without roots:
Bes, son of Nanammovvezz; Bliesblituth
that wild buffoon throned in an oaken booth;
wary Edarnon; brilliant Usconbuts;
Canutulachama who read the stars.
Where their fame flashed from, went to, is unknown.
The terror of their warriors is known,
naked, tattooed on every part (the hairs
of the groin are shaved on greatest fighters,
the fine bone needle dipped in dark-blue woad
rings the flesh with tender quick assurance:
he is *diuperr cartait*, rich pin; writers
like us regain mere pain on that blue road,
they think honour comes with the endurance.)

Colloquy in Glaschu

God but *le son du cor*, Columba sighed
to Kentigern, *est triste au fond silvarum!*
Frater, said Kentigern, I see no harm.
J'aime le son du cor, when day has died,
deep in the *bois*, and oystercatchers rise
before the fowler as he trudges home
and *sermo lupi* loosens the grey loam.
À l'horizon lointain is paradise,
abest silentium, le cor éclate –
– *et meurt*, Columba mused, but Kentigern
replied, *renaît et se prolonge*. The cell
is filled with song. Outside, *puer cantat*.
Veni venator sings the gallus kern.
The saints dip startled cups in Mungo's well.

Memento

over the cliff-top and into the mist
across the heather and down to the peat
here with the sheep and where with the peeweet
through the stubble and by the pheasant's tryst
above the pines and past the northern lights
along the voe and out to meet the ice
among the stacks and round their kreidekreis
in summer lightning and beneath white nights
behind the haar and in front of the tower
beyond the moor and against writ and ring
below the mort-gate and outwith all kind
under the hill and at the boskless bower
over the hills and far away to bring
over the hills and far away to mind

Matthew Paris

'North and then north and north again we sailed,
not that God is in the north or the south
but that the north is great and strange, a mouth
of baleen filtering the unknown, veiled
spoutings and sportings, curtains of white cold.
I made a map, I made a map of it.
Here I have bristly Scotland, almost split
in two, what sea-lochs and rough marches, old
forts, new courts, when Alexander their king
is dead will they live in love and peace, get
bearings, trace mountains, count stars, take capes, straits
in their stride as well as crop and shop, bring
luck home? *Pelagus vastissimum et
invium*, their element, my margin, waits.'

At Stirling Castle, 1507

Damian, D'Amiens, Damiano –
we never found out his true name, but there
he crouched, swarthy, and slowly sawed the air
with large strapped-on bat-membrane wings. Below
the battlements, a crowd prepared to jeer.
He frowned, moved back, and then with quick crow struts
ran forward, flapping strongly, whistling cuts
from the grey heavy space with his black gear
and on a huge spring and a cry was out
beating into vacancy, three, four, five,
till the crawling scaly Forth and the rocks
and the upturned heads replaced that steel shout
of sky he had replied to – left alive,
and not the last key snapped from high hard locks.

Thomas Young, M.A. (St Andrews)
for J.C.B.

'Yes, I taught Milton. He was a sharp boy.
He never understood predestination,
but then who does, within the English nation?
I did my best to let him see what joy
there must be in observing the damnation
of those whom God makes truly reprobate:
the fair percentage does not decreate
heaven, but gives all angels the elation
they are justly decreed to have deserved.
We took a short tour up to Auchterarder,
where there are strong sound sergeants of the creed,
but John could only ask how God was served
by those who neither stand nor wait, their ardour
rabid (he said) to expunge virtue's seed?'

Lady Grange on St Kilda

'They say I'm mad, but who would not be mad
on Hirta, when the winter raves along
the bay and howls through my stone hut, so strong
they thought I was and so I am, so bad
they thought I was and beat me black and blue
and banished me, my mouth of bloody teeth
and banished me to live and cry beneath
the shriek of sea-birds, and eight children too
we had, my lord, though I know what you are,
sleekit Jacobite, showed you up, you bitch,
and screamed outside your close at Niddry's Wynd,
until you set your men on me, and far
I went from every friend and solace, which
was cruel, out of mind, out of my mind.'

Theory of the Earth

James Hutton that true son of fire who said
to Burns 'Aye, man, the rocks melt wi the sun'
was sure the age of reason's time was done:
what but imagination could have read
granite boulders back to their molten roots?
And how far back was back, and how far on
would basalt still be basalt, iron iron?
Would second seas re-drown the fossil brutes?
'We find no vestige of a beginning,
no prospect of an end.' They died almost
together, poet and geologist,
and lie in wait for hilltop buoys to ring,
or aw the seas gang dry and Scotland's coast
dissolve in crinkled sand and pungent mist.

Poe in Glasgow

The sun beat on the Moby-Dick-browed boy.
It was a day to haunt the Broomielaw.
The smell of tar, the slap of water, draw
his heart out from the wharf in awe and joy.
Oh, not Virginia, not Liverpool –
and not the Isle of Dogs or Greenwich Reach –
but something through the masts – a blue – a beach –
an inland gorge of rivers green and cool.
'Wake up!' a sailor coiled with bright rope cried
and almost knocked him off his feet, making
towards his ship. 'You want to serve your time
as cabin-boy's assistant, eh?' The ride
and creak of wood comes home, testing, shaking.
'Where to?' He laughed. 'To Arnheim, boy, Arnheim!'

De Quincey in Glasgow

Twelve thousand drops of laudanum a day
kept him from shrieking. Wrapped in a duffle
buttoned to the neck, he made his shuffle,
door, table, window, table, door, bed, lay
on bed, sighed, groaned, jumped from bed, sat and wrote
till the table was white with pages, rang
for his landlady, ordered mutton, sang
to himself with pharmacies in his throat.
When afternoons grew late, he feared and longed
for dusk. In that high room in Rottenrow
he looks out east to the Necropolis.
Its crowded tombs rise jostling, living, thronged
with shadows, and the granite-bloodying glow
flares on the dripping bronze of a used kris.

Peter Guthrie Tait, Topologist

Leith dock's lashed spars roped the young heart of Tait.
What made gales tighten, not undo, each knot?
Nothing's more dazzling than a ravelling plot.
Stubby crisscrossing fingers fixed the freight
so fast he started sketching on the spot.
The mathematics of the twisted state
uncoiled its waiting elegances, straight.
Old liquid chains that strung the gorgeous tot
God spliced the mainbrace with, put on the slate,
and sent creation reeling from, clutched hot
as caustic on Tait's brain when he strolled late
along the links and saw the stars had got
such gouts and knots of well-tied fire the mate
must sail out whistling to his stormy lot.

G.M. Hopkins in Glasgow
For J.A.M.R.

Earnestly nervous yet forthright, melted
by bulk and warmth and unimposed rough grace,
he lit a ready fuse from face to face
of Irish Glasgow. Dark tough tight-belted
drunken Fenian poor ex-Ulstermen
crouched round a brazier like a burning bush
and lurched into his soul with such a push
that British angels blanched in mid-amen
to see their soldier stumble like a Red.
Industry's pauperism singed his creed.
He blessed them, frowned, beat on his hands. The load
of coal-black darkness clattering on his head
half-crushed, half-fed the bluely burning need
that trudged him back along North Woodside Road.

1893

For P. McC.

A Slav philosopher in Stronachlachar:
Vladimir Solovyov looked down the loch.
The sun was shimmering on birk and sauch.
'This beats the fishy vennels of St Machar,'
he said, and added, 'Inversnaid tomorrow!'
A boatman rowing to him from infinity
turned out to be a boatwoman. 'Divinity!'
he cried, 'shake back your hair, and shake back sorrow!'
The boat was grounded, she walked past him singing.
To her, he was a man of forty, reading.
Within him the words mounted: 'Sing for me,
dancing like Wisdom before the Lord, bringing
your mazy unknown waters with you, seeding
the Northern Lights and churning up the sea!'

The Ticket

'There are two rivers: how can a drop go
from one stream to the next?' Gurdjieff was asked.
The unflummoxable master stretched, basked.
'It must buy a ticket,' he said. A row
of demons dragged the Inaccessible
Pinnacle through the centre of Glasgow,
barking out sweaty orders, pledged to show
it was bloody juggernaut-time, able
to jam shrieking children under crashed spires.
But soon that place began to recompose,
the film ran back, the walls stood, the cries died,
the demons faded to familiar fires.
In New York, Gurdjieff changed his caftan, chose
a grape, sat, smiled. 'They never paid their ride.'

North Africa

Why did the poets come to the desert?
They learned the meaning of an oasis,
the meaning of heat, fellahin's phrases,
tents behind the khamsin-blasted dannert.
We watched MacLean at the Ruweisat Ridge
giving a piercing look as he passed by
the fly-buzzed grey-faced dead; swivelled our eye
west through tank-strewn dune and strafed-out village
with Henderson; and Hay saw Bizerta
burn; Garioch was taken at Tobruk,
parched *Kriegsgefangener*, calm, reading *Shveik*;
Morgan ate sand, slept sand at El Ballah
while gangrened limbs dropped in the pail; Farouk
fed Fraser memorandums like a shrike.

Caledonian Antisyzygy

– Knock knock. – Who's there? – Doctor. – Doctor Who? – No,
just Doctor. – What's up Doc? – Stop, that's all cock.
– O.K. – Knock knock. – Who's there? – Doctor Who. – Doc-
tor Who who? – Doctor, who's a silly schmo?
– Right. Out! – Aw. – Well, last chance, come on. – Knock knock.
– Who's there? – Doctor Jekyll. – Doctor Jekyll
who? – Doctor, 'd ye kill Mr Hyde? – Pig-swill!
Nada! Rubbish! Lies! Garbage! Never! Schlock!
– Calm down, your turn. – Knock knock. – Who's there? – Doctor
Knox. – Doctor Knox who? – Doctor Knocks Box Talks,
Claims T.V. Favours Grim Duo, Burke, Hare.
– Right, join hands. Make sure the door is locked, or
nothing will happen. – Dark yet? – Cover clocks.
– Knock. – Listen! – Is there anybody there?

Travellers (1)

The universe is like a trampoline.
We chose a springy clump near Arrochar
and with the first jump shot past Barnard's Star.
The universe is like a tambourine.
We clashed a brace of planets as we swung
some rolling unknown ringing system up
above our heads, and kicked it too. To sup,
sleep, recoup, we dropped to the House of Tongue.
The universe is like a trampoline.
Tongue threw us into a satellite bank.
We photographed a mole; a broch; the moon.
The universe is like a tambourine.
We stretched out, shook Saturn, its janglings sank
and leapt till it was neither night nor noon.

Travellers (2)

As it was neither night nor noon, we mused
a bit, dissolved ourselves a bit, took stock,
folded the play away and turned the lock.
Exhilarated travellers unused
to feeling blank can love the nescience
of a stilled moment. Undenied the time,
a lingering, a parasol, a lime.
There is no happiness in prescience,
and there is no regret in happiness.
A coast swept out in headlands and was lost.
And there we could have left the thought unthought
or hope undrafted, but that a bright press
of lights showed where a distant liner crossed.
Its horn blew through us, urgent, deep, unsought.

Seferis on Eigg

The isles of Scotland! the isles of Scotland!
But Byron sang elsewhere; loved, died elsewhere.
Seferis stiffly cupped warm blue May air
and slowly sifted it from hand to hand.
It was good and Greek. Amazed to find it,
he thought the dancing sea, the larks, the boats
spoke out as clear as from Aegean throats.
What else there was – he might half-unwind it.
One day he visited the silent cave
where Walter Scott, that tawdry Ulysses,
purloined a suffocated clansman's skull.
Crowns of Scottish kings were sacred; the lave
can whistle for dignity – who misses
them, peasants, slaves? Greeks, too, could shrug the cull.

Matt McGinn

We cannot see it, it keeps changing so.
All round us, *in and out, above, below,*
at evening, *phantom figures come and go,*
silently, *just a magic shadow show.*
A hoarse voice singing *come love watch with me*
was all we heard on that fog-shrouded bank.
We thought we saw him, but if so, he sank
into the irrecoverable sea.
Dear merry man, what is your country now?
Does it keep changing? Will we ever see it?
A crane, a backcourt, an accordion?
Or sherbet dabs, henna, and jasmined brow?
The book is clasped, and time will never free it.
Mektub. The caravan winds jangling on.

Post-Referendum

'No no, it will not do, it will not be.
I tell you you must leave your land alone.
Who do you think is poised to ring the phone?
Fish your straitjacket packet from the sea
you threw it in, get your headphones mended.
You don't want the world now, do you? Come on,
you're pegged out on your heathery futon,
take the matches from your lids, it's ended.'
We watched the strong sick dirkless Angel groan,
shiver, half-rise, batter with a shrunk wing
the space the Tempter was no longer in.
He tried to hear feet, calls, car-doors, shouts, drone
of engines, hooters, hear a meeting sing.
A coin clattered at the end of its spin.

Gangs

Naw naw, there's nae big wurds here, there ye go.
Christ man ye're in a bad wey, kin ye staun?
See here noo, wance we know jist where we're gaun,
we'll jump thon auld – stoap that, will ye – *Quango*.
Thaim that squealt *Lower Inflation*, aye, thaim,
plus thae *YY Zero Wage Increase* wans,
they'll no know what hit thim. See yours, and Dan's,
and mine's, that's three chibs. We'll soon hiv a team.
Whit's that? *Non-Index-Linked!* Did ye hear it?
Look! *Tiny Global Recession!* C'moan then,
ya bams, Ah'll take ye. *Market Power fae Drum!*
Dave, man, get up. Dave! Ach, ye're no near it.
Ah'm oan ma tod. But they'll no take a len
a me, Ah'm no deid yet, or deif, or dumb!

After a Death

A writer needs nothing but a table.
His pencil races, pauses, crosses out.
Five years ago he lost his friend, without
him he struggles through a different fable.
The one who died, he is the better one.
The other one is selfish, ruthless, he
uses people, floats in an obscure sea
of passions, half-drowns as the livid sun
goes down, calls out for help he will not give.
Examine yourself! He is afraid to.
But that is not quite true, I saw him look
into that terrible place, let him live
at least with what is eternally due
to love that lies in earth in cold Carluke.

Not the Burrell Collection

The Buenos Aires Vase, one mile across,
flickering with unsleeping silent flames,
its marble carved in vine-leaves mixed with names,
shirtless ones and *desaparecidos*;
a collier's iron collar, riveted,
stamped by his Burntisland owner; a spade
from Babiy Yar; a blood-crust from the blade
that jumped the corpse of Wallace for his head;
the stout rack soaked in Machiavelli's sweat;
a fire-circled scorpion; a blown frog;
the siege of Beirut in stained glass; a sift
of Auschwitz ash; an old tapestry-set
unfinished, with a crowd, a witch, a log;
a lachrymatory no man can lift.

1983

'A parrot Edward Lear drew has just died.'
There was a young lady of Corstorphine
who adopted a psittacine orphan.
It shrieked and it cried: they threw far and wide
her ashes right over Corstorphine. Zoos
guard and pamper the abandoned squawkers,
tickle stories from the raunchy talkers,
shoulder a bold centenarian muse
over artists deaf as earth. 'Oho! Lear
sketched me, delirious old man, how he
shuffled about, his tabby on the sill,
a stew on the stove, a brush in his ear,
and sometimes hummed, or he buzzed like a bee,
painting parrots and all bright brave things still!'

A Place of Many Waters

Infinitely variable water,
let seals bob in your silk or loll on Mull
where the lazy fringes rustle; let hull
and screw slew you round, blind heavy daughter
feeling for shores; keep kelpies in loch lairs,
eels gliding, malts mashing, salmon springing;
let the bullers roar to the terns winging
in from a North Sea's German Ocean airs
of pressing crashing Prussian evening blue;
give linns long fall; bubble divers bravely
down to mend the cable you love to rust;
and slant at night through lamplit cities, true
as change is true, on gap-site pools, gravely
splintering the puckering of the gust.

The Poet in the City

Rain stockaded Glasgow; we paused, changed gears,
found him solitary but cheerful in
Anniesland, with the cheerfulness you'd win,
we imagined, through schiltrons of banked fears.
The spears had a most sombre glint, as if
the forced ranks had re-closed, but there he wrote
steadily, with a peg for the wet coat
he'd dry and put on soon. Gulls cut the cliff
of those houses, we watched him follow them
intently, see them beat and hear them scream
about the invisible sea they smelt
and fish-white boats they raked from stern to stem
although their freedom was in fact his dream
of freedom with all guilts all fears unfelt.

The Norn (1)

It was high summer, and the sun was hot.
We flew up over Perthshire, following
Christo's great-granddaughter in her swing-wing
converted crop-sprayer till plastic shot
above Schiehallion from her spinneret
Scotland-shaped and Scotland-sized, descended
silent, tough, translucent, light-attended,
catching that shoal of contours in one net.
Beneath it, what amazement; anger; some
stretching in wonder at a sky to touch;
chaos at airports, stunned larks, no more rain!
It would not burn, it would not cut. The hum
of civic protest probed like Dali's crutch.
Children ran wild under that counterpane.

The Norn (2)

But was it art? We asked the French, who said
La nature est un temple où les vivants
sont les piliers, which was at least not wrong
but did it answer us? Old Christo's head
rolled from its box, wrapped in rough manila.
'The pillars of the temple are the dead,'
it said, 'packed up and bonded into lead.'
Jowls of hemp smelt sweet like crushed vanilla.
But his descendant in her flying-suit
carefully put the head back in its place.
'Of course it's art', she said, 'we just use men.
Pygmalion got it inside out, poor brute.
For all they've been made art, they've not lost face.
They'll lift the polythene, be men again'.

The Target

Then they were running with fire in their hair,
men and women were running anywhere,
women and children burning everywhere,
ovens of death were falling from the air.
Lucky seemed those at the heart of the blast
who left no flesh or ash or blood or bone,
only a shadow on dead Glasgow's stone,
when the black angel had gestured and passed.
Rhu was a demons' pit, Faslane a grave;
the shattered basking sharks that thrashed Loch Fyne
were their killer's tocsin: 'Where I am, watch;
when I raise one arm to destroy, I save
none; increase, multiply; vengeance is mine;
in no universe will man find his match.'

After Fallout

A giant gannet buzzed our glinty probe.
Its forty-metre wing-span hid the sun.
Life was stirring, the fallout time was done.
From *a stick-nest in Ygdrasil* the globe
was hatching genes like rajahs' koh-i-noors.
Over St Kilda, house-high poppy-beds
made forests; towering sea-pinks turned the heads
of even master mariners with lures
that changed the white sea-graves to scent-drenched groves.
Fortunate Isles! The gannet bucked our ship
with a quick sidelong swoop, clapped its wings tight,
dived, and exploding through the herring droves
dragged up a flailing manta by the lip
and flew it, twisting slowly, out of sight.

The Age of Heracleum

The jungle of Gleneagles was a long
shadow on our right as we travelled down.
Boars rummaged through the ballroom's toppled crown
of chandeliers and mashed the juicy throng
of giant hogweed stalks. Wild tramps with sticks
glared, kept a rough life. South in Fife we saw
the rusty buckled bridges, the firth raw
with filth and flower-heads, dead fish, dark slicks.
We stood in what had once been Princes Street.
Hogweed roots thrust, throbbed underneath for miles.
The rubble of the shops became the food
of new cracks running mazes round our feet,
and west winds blew, past shattered bricks and tiles,
millions of seeds through ruined Holyrood.

Computer Error: Neutron Strike

No one was left to hear the long All Clear.
Hot wind swept through the streets of Aberdeen
and stirred the corpse-clogged harbour. Each machine,
each building, tank, car, college, crane, stood sheer
and clean but that a shred of skin, a hand,
a blackened child driven like tumbleweed
would give the lack of ruins leave to feed
on horrors we were slow to understand
but did. Boiling fish-floating seas slopped round
the unmanned rigs that flared into the night;
the videos ran on, sham death, sham love;
the air-conditioners kept steady sound.
An automatic foghorn, and its light,
warned out to none below, and none above.

Inward Bound

Flapping, fluttering, like imploding porridge
being slowly uncooked on anti-gas,
the Grampians were a puny shrinking mass
of cairns and ski-tows sucked back to their origins. Pylons rumbled downwards; lighthouses
hissed into bays; reactors popped, ate earth.
We watched a fissure struggling with the girth
of old Glamis, but down it went. Boots, blouses,
hats, hands above heads, like feet-first divers
all those inhabitants pressed in to meet
badgers and stalactites, and to build in reverse
tenements deepest for late arrivers,
and domes to swim in, not to echo feet
or glow down, dim, on the draped, chanted hearse.

The Desert

There was a time when everything was sand.
It drifted down from Findhorn, south south south
and sifted into eye and ear and mouth
on battlefield or bed or plough-bent land.
Loose wars grew sluggish, and the bugles choked.
We saw some live in caves, and even tombs.
Mirages rose from dry Strathspey in plumes.
Scorpions appeared. Heaven's fires were stoked.
But soon they banded to bind dunes in grass,
made cactus farms, ate lizards, sank their wells.
They had their rough strong songs, rougher belief.
Did time preserve them through that narrow pass?
Or are they Guanches under conquerors' spells,
chiselled on sorry plinths in Tenerife?

The Coin

We brushed the dirt off, held it to the light.
The obverse showed us *Scotland*, and the head
of a red deer; the antler-glint had fled
but the fine cut could still be felt. All right:
we turned it over, read easily *One Pound*,
but then the shock of Latin, like a gloss,
Respublica Scotorum, sent across
such ages as we guessed but never found
at the worn edge where once the date had been
and where as many fingers had gripped hard
as hopes their silent race had lost or gained.
The marshy scurf crept up to our machine,
sucked at our boots. Yet nothing seemed ill-starred.
And least of all the realm the coin contained.

The Solway Canal

Slowly through the Cheviot hills at dawn
we sailed. The high steel bridge at Carter Bar
passed over us in fog with not a car
in its broad lanes. Our hydrofoil slid on,
vibrating quietly through wet rock walls
and scarves of dim half-sparkling April mist;
a wizard with a falcon on his wrist
was stencilled on our bow. Rough waterfalls
flashed on that northern island of the Scots
as the sun steadily came up and cast
red light along the uplands and the waves,
and gulls with open beaks tore out our thoughts
through the thick glass to where the Eildons massed,
or down to the Canal's drowned borderers' graves.

A Scottish Japanese Print

Lighter and lighter, not eternity,
only a morning breaking on dark fields.
The sleepers might almost throw back those shields,
jump to stations as if golden pity
could probe the grave, the beauty was so great
in that silent slowly brightening place.
No, it is the living who wait for grace,
the hare, the fox, the farmer at the gate.
And Glasgow's windows took the strong spring sun
in the corner of a water-meadow,
its towers shadowed by a pigeon's flight.
Not daisy-high, children began to run
like tumbling jewels, as in old Yeddo,
and with round eyes unwound their wild red kite.

Outward Bound

– That was the time Scotland began to move.
– Scotland move? No, it is impossible!
– It became an island, and was able
to float in the Atlantic lake and prove
crannogs no fable. Like a sea-washed log
it loved to tempt earnest geographers,
duck down and dub them drunk hydrographers,
shake itself dry, no longer log but dog.
– Was it powered? On stilts? – Amazing grace
was found in granite, it moved on pure sound.
Greenland twisted round to hear it, Key West
whistled, waved, Lanzarote's ashy face
cracked open with laughter. There was no ground
of being, only being, sweetest and best.

On Jupiter

Scotland was found on Jupiter. That's true.
We lost all track of time, but there it was.
No one told us its origins, its cause.
A simulacrum, a dissolving view?
It seemed as solid as a terrier
shaking itself dry from a brisk black swim
in the reservoir of Jupiter's grim
crimson trustless eye. No soul-ferrier
guarded the swampy waves. Any gods there,
if they had made the thing in play, were gone,
and if the land had launched its own life out
among the echoes of inhuman air,
its launchers were asleep, or had withdrawn,
throwing their stick into a sea of doubt.

Clydegrad

It was so fine we lingered there for hours.
The long broad streets shone strongly after rain.
Sunset blinded the tremble of the crane
we watched from, dazed the heliport-towers.
The mile-high buildings flashed, flushed, greyed, went dark,
greyed, flushed, flashed, chameleons under flak
of cloud and sun. The last far thunder-sack
ripped and spilled its grumble. Ziggurat-stark,
a power-house reflected in the lead
of the old twilight river leapt alive
lit up at every window, and a boat
of students rowed past, slid from black to red
into the blaze. But where will they arrive
with all, boat, city, earth, like them, afloat?

A Golden Age

That must have been a time of happiness.
The air was mild, the Campsie Fells had vines.
Dirigible parties left soft sky-signs
and bursts of fading music. Who could guess
what they might not accomplish, they had seas
in cities, cities in the sea; their domes
and crowded belvederes hung free, their homes
eagle-high or down among whitewashed quays.
And women sauntered often with linked arms
through night streets, or alone, or danced a maze
with friends. Perhaps it did not last. What lasts?
The bougainvillea millenniums
may come and go, but then in thistle days
a strengthened seed outlives the hardest blasts.

The Summons

The year was ending, and the land lay still.
Despite our countdown, we were loath to go,
kept padding along the ridge, the broad glow
of the city beneath us, and the hill
swirling with a little mist. Stars were right,
plans, power; only now this unforeseen
reluctance, like a slate we could not clean
of characters, yet could not read, or write
our answers on, or smash, or take with us.
Not a hedgehog stirred. We sighed, climbed in, locked.
If it was love we felt, would it not keep,
and travel where we travelled? Without fuss
we lifted off, but as we checked and talked
a far horn grew to break that people's sleep.